the ULTIMATE FESTIVE FEAST

the ULTIMATE FESTIVE FEAST

With recipes from your favourite chefs

from
factory
to store
we're
your
charity

caravan®

This book was produced for Caravan, the trading name of the National Grocers Benevolent Fund, a registered charity no. 1095897 (England & Wales) & SCO 39255 (Scotland).
The charity is a company limited by guarantee, registered in England & Wales no. 4620683.

1 2 3 4 5 6 7 8 9 10

Published in 2011 by Ebury Press, an imprint of Ebury Publishing

A Random House Group Company

The Random House Group Limited Reg. No. 954009

Addresses for companies within the Random House Group can be found at www.randomhouse.co.uk

A CIP catalogue record for this book is available from the British Library

The Random House Group Limited supports The Forest Stewardship Council (FSC®), the leading international forest certification organisation. Our books carrying the FSC label are printed on FSC® certified paper. FSC is the only forest certification scheme endorsed by the leading environmental organisations, including Greenpeace. Our paper procurement policy can be found at www.randomhouse.co.uk/environment.

To buy books by your favourite authors and register for offers visit www.randomhouse.co.uk

Project editor: Patricia Burgess
Art direction and design: Smith & Gilmour
Food photography: Dan Jones (but David Loftus, pp. 115, 137)
Food stylists: Sonja Edridge, Emma Lahaye and Danny Maguire
Stylist: Rachel Jukes

Printed and bound by Butler, Tanner & Dennis Ltd, Frome and London

ISBN 9780091945107

NOTE
Unless specified otherwise:
* Onions, garlic and vegetables should be peeled or trimmed and washed before use.
* All spoon measures are level.
* Eggs are medium (size 3).

CONTENTS

FOREWORD

Thank you for purchasing *The Ultimate Festive Feast*.

This fantastic collection of seasonal recipes will see you through
the festive period in the most delicious way possible, and hold your hand
through all the planning and preparation. We are immensely grateful to
all the chefs who contributed so generously to the book: Mary Berry,
Ainsley Harriott, Angela Hartnett, James Martin, Jamie Oliver, Gordon Ramsay,
Michel Roux Sr and Michel Roux Jr. Proceeds from the sale of this book
will go to support the work of Caravan, the charity for the grocery industry.

Caravan is a long-established benevolent society that can trace its
origins back to the 1850s. The charity offers current and former industry
colleagues both financial and emotional support in their time of need. Caravan
is only able to do this thanks to the support of the grocery industry, which
raises money for the charity through a variety of fundraising events and
initiatives, donations and corporate sponsorship.

The help that Caravan provides makes a real difference
to real lives. You can find out more about the role of the
charity at www.caravan-charity.org.uk

Merry Christmas and a Happy New Year!

Gillian Barker
DIRECTOR GENERAL OF CARAVAN

CHRISTMAS
COUNTDOWN

No matter how much time we have to prepare for Christmas, it never seems enough, does it? There's so much to think about, so much to buy, so much to make. Of course, we always get through it and swear next year will be different — less fraught, better organised — but how often do we manage that?

This year there's no excuse. Simply follow the timetable here and your Christmas preparation will go like clockwork.

6

OCTOBER

* Make Christmas chutney (page 132)

5

NOVEMBER

* Make Christmas cake (page 185)
* 'Feed' Christmas cake with brandy at weekly intervals
* Make Christmas pudding (page 156) — traditionally made on Stir-up Sunday, about four weeks before Christmas

4

EARLY DECEMBER

* Plan your menus (pages 220, 221)
* Make a shopping list and start stocking up
* Order your turkey, ham and other joints

Make freezer meals and side dishes, such as:
* Venison casserole (page 67)
* Cheese and ham pie (page 78)
* Carrot and coriander roulade (page 107)
* Vegetarian lasagne (page 110)
* Parsnip purée (page 122)

Make freezable puddings and bakes, such as:
* Christmas ice cream (page 183)
* Blood orange and Cointreau sorbet (page 168)
* Raspberry granita (page 167)
* Ultimate chocolate roulade (page 193)
* Cranberry mince pies (page 194)
* Cranberry and apricot fruit cake (page 188)

Make and store in an airtight container:
* Iced gingerbread (page 187)
* Christmas biscuits (page 197)
* Florentines (page 198)

(3) CHRISTMAS WEEK

* Prepare your Christmas ham
* Decorate Christmas cake

(2) CHRISTMAS EVE

* Collect fresh turkey
* Make gravy stock (page 41) and stuffing
* Make Cranberry sauce and Bread sauce (page 131)
* Make Brandy butter (page 156)
* Defrost mince pies
* Parboil potatoes for roasting
* Set out Christmas muffin ingredients (page 184)

(1) CHRISTMAS DAY

(assuming you plan to eat a 5 kg turkey at 2 p.m.)

9.00 Make Christmas muffins (page 184)

10.30 Preheat oven and stuff turkey (page 40)

10.45 Put prepared turkey in oven (2¾ hours plus 30 minutes' rest)
Prepare the vegetables and sausages wrapped in bacon
Select your wine. Put white wine in the fridge to chill; open red wine to breathe

12.30 Heat fat in a roasting pan and put parboiled potatoes in to roast
Add wrapped sausages to turkey tin

1.15 Start steaming pudding(s)

1.30 Transfer turkey and sausages to a warm carving plate, cover with foil and leave to rest
Boil water for veg

1.45 Cook sprouts and any other veg
Reheat bread sauce
Make gravy with giblet stock (page 41)
Put cooked food and sauces in serving dishes
Carve turkey

2.00 Tuck in

1

STARTERS

*Get your festive celebrations off to
a delicious start with some of the superb
recipes in this section. From soups and
salads to pâtés, mousses, tarts and terrines,
there's something for every occasion.*

Butternut squash and chorizo soup

SERVES 6

Warming, rich and satisfying, this is a heart-warming soup to welcome you home on a winter's day. When in season, the butternut squash can easily be replaced with pumpkin, which gives a creamy finish.

1 kg butternut squash, deseeded
4 red Romero peppers or
   3 ordinary red peppers,
   deseeded
4 tbsp olive oil
2 celery sticks, roughly chopped
2 onions, roughly chopped
2 garlic cloves, finely chopped
400 g potatoes, chopped
2 tsp dried oregano
2 tsp sweet paprika
pinch chilli flakes
1 tbsp sherry vinegar,
   plus extra to serve (optional)
1 litre vegetable stock
75 g chorizo
salt and freshly ground
   black pepper

ROUGHLY CHOP THE SQUASH AND PEPPERS, reserving a quarter of the peppers and about 75 g of the squash. Heat 3 tablespoons of the olive oil in a large pan over a medium heat. Add the squash, peppers, celery, onions, garlic and potato and leave to soften, partially covered, for 10 minutes.

ADD THE OREGANO, PAPRIKA, chilli flakes, sherry vinegar (if using) and stock. Add seasoning and bring to the boil. Lower the heat and simmer for 20 minutes.

ABOUT 5 MINUTES BEFORE THE END of the cooking time, chop the reserved pepper and squash and the chorizo into small pieces. Heat a small frying pan and cook these chopped ingredients for 10 minutes over a medium heat, stirring until the squash is golden.

CHECK THE SEASONING and serve the soup topped with the chorizo and vegetable garnish, and an extra drizzle of sherry vinegar if you wish. If you prefer a smooth soup, purée the contents of the saucepan with a stick blender.

Carrot, chestnut and coriander soup

SERVES 6—8

Here is a chunky soup made with homemade stock and flavoured with coriander for a really intense, warming flavour.

350 g vacuum-packed
    chestnuts
900 g carrots
2 leeks
50 g butter
1 tbsp ground coriander
pinch of sugar
4 tbsp chopped fresh coriander
salt and freshly ground pepper

For the stock
2 onions
2 cloves
3 carrots
2 celery sticks, with leaves
1 raw or cooked chicken
    carcass, plus giblets
2–3 parsley sprigs
1 bouquet garni (1 bay leaf tied
    together with a sprig of
    rosemary and thyme)
1 bay leaf
6 black peppercorns

FIRST MAKE THE STOCK. Halve the unpeeled onions vertically and stud with the cloves. Chop the carrots roughly without peeling. Roughly chop the celery. Place all the vegetables in a large saucepan with the chicken carcass, giblets if available (excluding liver), herbs and peppercorns. Cover with at least 2 litres cold water and bring slowly to the boil, skimming off any scum that rises to the surface. Lower the heat, half-cover and simmer for at least 1 hour. Strain the stock through a fine sieve and discard the chicken and vegetables. Cool, then remove any fat from the surface.

TO MAKE THE SOUP, chop the chestnuts roughly and reserve. Peel the carrots, then cut into medium chunks. Trim and slice the leeks into rounds.

MELT THE BUTTER IN A SAUCEPAN and add half the carrots, all the leeks and the ground coriander. Cook gently for about 5 minutes, until softened, then add 1.7 litres stock and the sugar. Half-cover and simmer for 20 minutes, until the vegetables are very tender.

MEANWHILE, COOK THE RESERVED CARROTS in a steamer or boiling salted water for 15—20 minutes, until tender. Drain and set aside.

PURÉE THE SOUP IN A BLENDER or food processor until smooth, then return to the pan. Stir in the reserved carrots, chestnuts and fresh coriander. Check the seasoning. Reheat until almost boiling.

POUR INTO WARMED SOUP BOWLS and serve with hot herb bread.

Pumpkin soup

SERVES 4

This is a fantastic autumnal soup. Adding a Parmesan rind to the pan when it's cooking gives a lovely depth of flavour. Although I think truffle oil has been over-exposed in recent years, a drop of it does finish off this soup very well. You can leave out the ceps if you prefer.

50 g butter
1 x 1 kg ripe pumpkin or butternut squash, peeled, deseeded and cut into 1.5 cm cubes
2 tbsp white wine
rind of Parmesan (about 50 g)
1 litre good chicken stock
drizzle of double cream (optional)
drizzle of truffle oil (optional)
salt and freshly ground black pepper

To serve (optional)
knob of butter
1 tbsp olive oil
100 g fresh ceps
handful of Parmesan shavings

HEAT THE 50 G OF BUTTER IN A LARGE PAN until melted. Add the pumpkin and lightly sauté over a low heat, stirring constantly to prevent sticking, for about 10 minutes. It should be soft but not coloured.

POUR IN THE WINE and allow it to bubble and reduce until completely evaporated. Cover with a lid and cook for 8–10 minutes, until the pumpkin is completely tender.

ADD THE PARMESAN RIND and all but 200 ml of the chicken stock to the pan and return to the boil. Once boiling, lower the heat and cook for a further 5 minutes. Remove and discard the Parmesan rind.

TAKE THE SOUP OFF THE HEAT and allow to cool a little before transferring it to a blender or food processor. Whizz until smooth, then pass through a fine sieve. If necessary, correct the consistency with a little more chicken stock or a touch of cream. Check the seasoning.

IF YOU ARE SERVING THE SOUP with the sautéd ceps, heat the butter and olive oil in a frying pan over a medium heat. Add the ceps and cook for 2–3 minutes, until golden. Season to taste.

REHEAT THE SOUP if necessary, then ladle into individual bowls. Add a drizzle of truffle oil, if liked, the sautéd ceps and a few Parmesan shavings.

Jerusalem artichoke and Parmesan soup

SERVES 6

The flavour of fresh Parmesan makes this soup really special. Don't be tempted to use the dry cheese sold in cartons — it bears no comparison to the real thing. Serve with the easy-to-make melba toast.

450 g Jerusalem artichokes
2 shallots
50 g butter
1 tsp mild curry paste
900 ml chicken or vegetable
    stock
150 ml single cream
    (or milk for a less rich soup)
freshly grated nutmeg, to taste
pinch of cayenne pepper
4 tbsp freshly grated Parmesan
    cheese
salt and freshly ground pepper

For the melba toast
3–4 slices day-old soft-grain
    white bread
freshly grated Parmesan cheese,
    for sprinkling
¼ tsp paprika

SCRUB THE JERUSALEM ARTICHOKES thoroughly to remove any dirt. Pat dry, then slice thinly. Peel and dice the shallots.

MELT THE BUTTER IN A LARGE SAUCEPAN and add the shallots. Cook gently for 5 minutes until soft and golden. Stir in the curry paste and cook for 1 minute. Add the sliced artichokes and stock; stir well. Bring to the boil, cover and simmer for about 15 minutes or until the artichokes are tender.

MEANWHILE, MAKE THE MELBA TOAST. Preheat the oven to 180°C/Gas 4. Toast the bread lightly on both sides. Quickly cut off the crusts and split each slice in half horizontally. Scrape off any doughy bits, then sprinkle with Parmesan and paprika. Place on a baking sheet and bake in the oven for 10–15 minutes or until uniformly golden.

ADD THE CREAM, NUTMEG AND CAYENNE to the soup. Transfer to a blender or food processor and work until smooth, then pass through a sieve into a clean saucepan. Reheat the soup and stir in the Parmesan cheese. Taste and adjust the seasoning. Serve at once, with the hot Melba toast.

Chicken liver and pistachio pâté

SERVES 8–10

Blended with cream cheese rather than butter, this tasty pâté gives a lighter and less calorific result. If you are concerned about calories, you could omit the butter seal altogether and instead decorate the top with chopped herbs.

2 streaky bacon rashers,
    derinded and finely chopped
700 g chicken livers
about 225 g butter
1 or 2 garlic cloves, chopped
large pinch of ground allspice
125 g flat mushrooms
1 medium onion
200 g low-fat soft cheese
2 tbsp double cream
40 g shelled pistachio nuts,
    plus a few extra for garnish
1 tbsp each chopped fresh
    parsley, chives and thyme
salt and freshly ground pepper
parsley or other herb leaves,
    to garnish

PLACE THE BACON in a heavy-based frying pan and heat gently until the fat starts to run, then increase the heat and cook until lightly browned.

MEANWHILE, TRIM THE CHICKEN LIVERS and remove any membranes and the white fibrous bits in the middle. Roughly chop the livers.

ADD 50 G OF THE BUTTER TO THE PAN and heat until it has melted. Add the livers with the garlic and allspice and cook briskly over a high heat until the livers are sealed and browned on the outside but still a little pink (not bloody) on the inside. Remove the bacon and livers from the pan with a slotted spoon and set aside.

FINELY CHOP THE MUSHROOMS AND ONION. Add to the pan and cook gently until the onion is softened. Remove from the heat.

TRANSFER THE LIVERS AND BACON to a blender. Add the onion and mushrooms, along with any butter remaining in the pan. Add the soft cheese and cream and work until smooth. Turn into a mixing bowl.

ROUGHLY CHOP THE NUTS, then fold into the pâté, along with the herbs. Season to taste. Spoon the pâté into ramekins or one large dish and level the top.

MELT THE REMAINING BUTTER over a very low heat. Slowly pour into a jug, leaving the sediment behind. Carefully pour the clarified butter over the pâté. (Depending on the size of your dishes, you might need to melt a little more than suggested.) Arrange the herbs and pistachios for garnish in the liquid butter. Chill overnight. Serve with plenty of good bread or toast.

MICHEL ROUX JR

Rabbit terrine cooked in Chablis with grain mustard

SERVES 8

A favourite in the Roux household and at Le Gavroche, this terrine is delicious with hot sourdough toast.

1 x 1.5 kg rabbit
   (domestic, not wild)
2 tbsp olive oil
1 carrot, diced
1 onion, diced
100 g smoked bacon, diced
400 ml Chablis wine
½ calf's foot, split in two
2 bay leaves
1 thyme sprig
1 litre chicken stock
2 tbsp grain mustard
generous handful flatleaf
   parsley, tarragon and chervil,
   roughly chopped
salt and freshly ground pepper

PREHEAT THE OVEN to 120°C/Gas ½.

PREPARE THE RABBIT by removing the heart and lungs, but if you like the liver and kidneys, leave them in to cook with the rabbit.

HEAT THE OIL in a large casserole and fry the rabbit to seal on all sides. Add the carrot, onion and bacon and cook over a medium heat until lightly coloured.

ADD THE WINE and boil for 1 minute, then add the calf's foot, bay leaves, thyme and stock. Season with salt and freshly ground pepper. Bring to the boil, cover with a lid and cook in the oven for 1½ hours.

REMOVE FROM THE OVEN and leave to cool until hand hot. Now pick all the meat off the bones and shred between your fingers into a bowl.

PASS THE COOKING LIQUID through a colander into a pan. Return the carrot and onion to the meat. Boil the cooking liquid and skim thoroughly to remove as much fat and scum as possible; reduce by a third and pour over the meat.

STIR IN THE MUSTARD AND HERBS, taste and adjust the seasoning. Pour into a porcelain terrine, then cover and refrigerate for at least 12 hours.

SERVE WITH TOASTED SOURDOUGH BREAD and a little salad of chives, chervil, tarragon, watercress, wild rocket and dandelion dressed in red wine vinegar and a rich olive oil.

ANGELA
HARTNETT

Mackerel with filo pastry

SERVES 4

The mackerel used here needs to be extremely fresh, as it's barely cooked when served. You can assemble these little open pastries ahead of time and pop in the oven later.

4 x 90 g fresh mackerel fillets, skinned and pin-boned
500 g vine-ripened tomatoes
100 g butter
7 sheets of filo pastry
olive oil, for drizzling
salt and freshly ground pepper

PREHEAT THE OVEN to 180°C/Gas 4.

SLICE EACH MACKEREL FILLET into 6 thin pieces.

TO PREPARE THE TOMATOES, make a little incision with a sharp knife in the top of each one. Bring a pan of salted water to the boil and blanch the tomatoes in it for 10 seconds. Drain and transfer immediately to a bowl of iced water – this will make the skins easier to remove. Peel, quarter and deseed the tomatoes, then cut the flesh into 5 mm squares. Set aside.

HEAT THE BUTTER in a small pan over a low heat, making sure it does not boil. Remove from the direct heat and leave to rest in a warm place on the hob for 10 minutes. At this point it should separate into three layers. Skim off and discard the top layer. Strain what's left to remove the bottom layer.

LAY A SHEET OF FILO PASTRY on a baking sheet, keeping the rest of the pastry covered with a damp cloth to prevent it drying out. Brush with the clarified butter and top with another sheet of filo. Continue the process with the remaining 5 sheets, finishing with a plain sheet of filo. Bake in the preheated oven for 10 minutes, then set aside to cool.

CUT THE PASTRY into 4 rectangles measuring about 10 x 6 cm. Scatter a quarter of the tomatoes over each piece and arrange the mackerel slices on top. Drizzle with a little olive oil, season and bake for 5–7 minutes, or until the fish is just cooked.

Crab salad

SERVES 8

For this recipe you will need the white meat from two freshly cooked crabs, each about 1.4 kg (freeze the brown meat for future use). Failing that, use frozen white meat, defrosted and well drained.

450 g white crab meat, fresh
   or frozen and thawed
6 spring onions, trimmed
2 tbsp chopped fresh coriander
1 tbsp chopped fresh chives
pinch of cayenne pepper
2 garlic cloves
2.5 cm piece fresh root ginger,
   peeled
2 tbsp sunflower oil
2 lime leaves, shredded
½ tsp dried crushed chilli flakes
4 tbsp lime juice
1 tbsp sugar
1 tsp shrimp paste (optional)
1 tbsp Thai fish sauce or
   soy sauce
1–2 heads of radicchio or
   red chicory
50 g cucumber
25 g beansprouts

To garnish
lime wedges
coriander sprigs

FLAKE THE WHITE CRAB MEAT into shreds and place in a bowl. Finely chop the spring onions and add to the crab with the coriander, chives and cayenne pepper. Mix gently, then cover and chill until required.

USING A PESTLE AND MORTAR or spice grinder, crush the garlic and ginger together. Heat the oil in a small pan, add the garlic, ginger, lime leaves and chilli flakes and fry over a gentle heat for 3 minutes, until softened but not brown. Add the lime juice, sugar, shrimp paste (if using) and the fish sauce. Stir well, then remove from the heat. Leave until cold.

DRIZZLE THE COOLED DRESSING over the crab mixture and toss lightly until evenly combined. Arrange the radicchio or chicory leaves on serving plates and spoon in the crab mixture. Thinly slice the cucumber and arrange on top of each serving with the beansprouts. Garnish with lime wedges and coriander sprigs to serve.

Smoked fish terrine

SERVES 6

A pretty white and pink-flecked mousse, this is flavoured with a hint of orange. To complement the smoky flavour and cut through the saltiness, the mousse is best served with a sharp, crunchy salad, such as sliced orange and chicory dressed with olive oil and orange juice. Accompany with warm toasted bread.

225 g undyed smoked white fish, such as haddock, cod, halibut
1 tsp finely grated orange rind
2 tsp orange juice
freshly ground white pepper
225 g smoked salmon
2 egg whites, chilled
150 ml whipping cream, chilled
dill sprigs, to garnish

CUT UP THE WHITE FISH and remove any bones with tweezers. Place in a food processor or blender with the orange rind, orange juice and plenty of pepper. Blend until smooth. Cover the processor bowl and chill in the freezer for 10 minutes.

MEANWHILE, roughly chop the smoked salmon. Lightly oil or butter a 900 ml terrine and line the base with greaseproof paper. Preheat the oven to 180°C/ Gas 4.

TRANSFER THE BOWL from the freezer to the processor. With the machine running, add the egg whites through the feeder tube, then add the cream; do not overwork or the mixture will curdle. Turn out into a bowl. Gently stir in the smoked salmon so that the mixture is flecked with pink.

CAREFULLY FILL the terrine with the mixture, packing it down well to exclude air pockets, then level the surface. Cover the terrine with buttered greaseproof paper and place in a roasting tin. Pour in enough boiling water to come halfway up the side. Bake in the preheated oven for 35—40 minutes, or until firm to the touch.

RUN A THIN-BLADED KNIFE around the inside of the terrine and unmould onto a warmed platter. Cut into slices and arrange on individual plates. Garnish with dill and serve warm.

Salmon tartlets

These little tarts, filled with a creamy salmon mixture, are grilled until deliciously melting. Serve on a bed of baby spinach leaves.

25 g butter
1 shallot, finely chopped
25 g plain flour
300 ml milk
1 egg yolk
275 g cooked salmon, flaked
1 tbsp chopped dill or parsley
salt and freshly ground pepper
1 tbsp lemon juice
baby spinach leaves, to serve
dill or parsley sprigs, to garnish

For the pastry
225 g plain flour
110 g butter
1 egg yolk (size 1)

For the hollandaise sauce
40 ml wine vinegar
3 peppercorns
1 bay leaf
1 blade of mace
1 egg yolk (size 1)
75 g butter
lemon juice

FIRST MAKE THE PASTRY. Sift the flour into a bowl and rub in the butter until the mixture resembles fine breadcrumbs. Add the egg yolk and a few drops of chilled water to mix to a smooth dough. Wrap in clingfilm and leave to rest in the fridge for 30 minutes.

PREHEAT THE OVEN to 190°C/Gas 5. Roll out the pastry and use to line 6 x 10 cm tart tins. Prick with a fork, then line with a square of foil. Fill with rice or dried beans. Place on a baking sheet and bake blind for 10 minutes. Remove the foil and rice or beans.

MEANWHILE, make the filling. Melt the butter in a pan, add the shallot and cook until softened. Add the flour and cook, stirring, for 30 seconds. Stir in the milk and slowly bring to the boil, stirring until thickened. Simmer for 2 minutes. Leave to cool.

ADD THE EGG YOLK to the sauce, then stir in the salmon and dill. Season with salt, pepper and lemon juice. Divide between the pastry cases and bake for 20 minutes, or until set.

MEANWHILE, make the hollandaise. Put the vinegar, peppercorns, bay leaf and mace in a small pan. Bring to the boil and boil steadily to reduce to 1 tablespoon.

CREAM THE EGG YOLK with a pinch of salt and a quarter of the butter. Place the bowl over a pan of simmering water and beat until slightly thickened. Strain in the reduced vinegar, then beat in the remaining butter a little at a time until the sauce has thickened. Season with salt, pepper and lemon juice.

SERVE THE TARTLETS with the hollandaise on the side.

Soft-boiled egg with smoked salmon, asparagus and caviar

SERVES 6

30 small asparagus tips
4 slices smoked salmon
2 tbsp double cream
2 tbsp horseradish
4 eggs
3 tbsp Sevruga caviar
olive oil
1 cylindrical brioche loaf, cut into 12 round slices about 1 cm thick and 3–5 cm wide
salt and freshly ground black pepper

PEEL THE ASPARAGUS and trim to 4 cm lengths. Cook in a pan of boiling salted water for 5–7 minutes, or until just tender. Refresh immediately in ice-cold water and drain well.

CUT THE SMOKED SALMON SLICES into 18 circles, using a cutter the same diameter as the brioche.

WHIP THE CREAM and add to the horseradish.

COOK THE EGGS in boiling water for 3½ minutes, then hold under cold running water for 10 seconds. Peel while still hot.

PUT THE EGGS INTO A WARM DISH and break them up with a fork (the yolks should be runny and the whites solid). Season with a little pepper and gently fold in the caviar.

REHEAT THE ASPARAGUS in a pan of boiling salted water. Drain and roll in a little olive oil to make the pieces glossy.

PUT A SMALL DOLLOP of the horseradish cream in the centre of each serving plate. Place a smoked salmon circle on top, then more horseradish and then a lightly toasted brioche slice. Repeat the layers to finish with a stack containing 2 brioche slices and 3 smoked salmon circles on each place.

ARRANGE THE ASPARAGUS on top and spoon on the egg and caviar mixture.

Fresh salmon mousse

SERVES 8

These loosely wrapped parcels of fresh and smoked salmon make an excellent prepare-ahead starter, whatever the occasion.

450 g salmon fillets or pieces
1 carrot
1 onion
1 bay leaf
150 ml fish stock
salt and freshly ground pepper
1½ tsp powdered gelatine
75 ml dry white wine
1 tbsp chopped fresh chives
    or tarragon
3 tbsp mayonnaise
150 ml double cream
8 slices smoked salmon
    (about 175 g in total)

To garnish
quails' eggs
fish eggs (optional)
tarragon sprigs

PLACE THE SALMON IN A PAN in which it fits quite snugly. Peel and roughly chop the carrot and onion. Add to the pan with the bay leaf, stock and seasoning. Bring to the boil, lower the heat and simmer very gently for 10 minutes, turning the salmon halfway through cooking.

DRAIN THE FISH, reserving the stock. Pull the flesh away from the bones, then roughly flake, discarding the skin and any stray bones. Strain the stock and set aside.

SPRINKLE THE GELATINE over the white wine in a small heatproof bowl and leave to soften for 5 minutes.

MEANWHILE, blend the fish in a food processor with the cooking juices until almost smooth. Transfer to a bowl.

STAND THE BOWL OF GELATINE in a pan of simmering water and leave until dissolved. Stir into the salmon mixture, then beat in the chives or tarragon and mayonnaise; season lightly.

WHIP THE CREAM until just holding its shape. Fold into the salmon mixture, using a large metal spoon. Turn the mousse into a container and chill for several hours or overnight, until softly set.

TO SERVE, lay the smoked salmon slices on a board. Place a spoonful of the mousse on each slice. Bring the ends of the salmon up over the mousse and twist together. Arrange on individual serving plates and garnish with quails' eggs, fish eggs (if desired) and tarragon sprigs.

Grilled avocado stuffed with crab

SERVES 4

Soft goats' cheese lends a mild, fresh taste and creamy texture to the crab meat. If available, choose small Hass avocados for their nutty flavour. Serve the stuffed avocados thickly sliced on a bed of crisp, colourful salad leaves, lightly dressed with olive oil and lemon juice.

125 g white crab meat
125 g fresh soft goats' cheese
1 tsp chopped tarragon
1 tbsp lemon juice
2 ripe avocados
50 g brown crab meat
2 plum tomatoes
salt and freshly ground pepper

For the dressing
1 tbsp walnut oil
2 tbsp olive oil
1 tbsp lemon juice

IN A BOWL, loosen the white crab meat with a fork, removing any pieces of shell. Add 50 g of the goats' cheese and the chopped tarragon. Mix together with a fork, seasoning to taste.

CUT THE AVOCADOS IN HALF and remove the stones. Brush the cut surfaces with lemon juice to prevent discoloration. Divide the brown crab meat between the four avocado halves, spooning it into the cavities.

DIVIDE THE WHITE CRAB meat mixture between the avocados, mounding it over the brown meat and spreading it over the avocado flesh.

SLICE THE TOMATOES THINLY and arrange over the crab. Crumble the remaining goats' cheese on top of the tomatoes and season with pepper.

PREHEAT THE GRILL TO MEDIUM. Place the avocados on a baking sheet or in an ovenproof dish and grill for about 10 minutes, until the cheese has browned and the avocado is warm.

WHISK THE DRESSING ingredients together in a small bowl, seasoning to taste.

TO SERVE, cut the avocados crosswise into thick slices and arrange on a bed of salad leaves. Drizzle with the dressing. Serve warm or cold.

Tiger prawns and feta on toast

SERVES 2

Although some people are horrified by the fusion of fish and cheese — especially the Italians, who baulk at tourists who ask for Parmesan on their linguine vongole — sweet plump prawns go brilliantly with salty feta. The mixture is delicious on thick slices of granary toast — the garlicky, buttery juices infuse with the aniseed tang of fennel, and the bread becomes irresistibly moist.

4 tbsp extra virgin olive oil
2 garlic cloves, halved
1 celery stick, finely sliced
1 tsp fennel seeds
225 g raw tiger prawns, peeled
juice of 1 lemon
100 g feta cheese, crumbled
4 slices granary bread
    (about 1.5 cm thick)

HEAT HALF THE OIL in a large frying pan over a high heat, add the garlic, celery and fennel seeds and fry for 2 minutes. Now add the prawns and fry for a further 2–3 minutes, until they turn pink. Tip into a mixing bowl and squeeze over the lemon juice. Crumble in the feta and give everything a good mix.

TOAST THE BREAD, divide equally between two plates and spoon the prawns and feta over the top.

French bean and omelette ribbon salad

SERVES 4

Thin strips of omelette festoon slim French beans in this pretty salad, which is enhanced by a punchy dressing full of Mediterranean flavours. Serve accompanied by olive bread.

2 eggs
50 ml olive oil
350 g French beans
1 large garlic clove
1 tsp red wine vinegar
1 tsp balsamic vinegar
2 sun-dried tomatoes,
   in oil, drained
1 tsp capers
salt and freshly ground pepper
olive bread, to serve

BREAK THE EGGS INTO A BOWL, add seasoning and beat lightly with a fork. Smear an 18–20 cm frying pan (preferably non-stick) with a little olive oil and place over a moderate heat. When it is hot, pour in half the egg mixture and swirl it around the pan to spread thinly. It will set almost immediately. Turn out onto a plate and repeat with the remaining egg, turning it out onto a separate plate.

TOP AND TAIL THE FRENCH BEANS and cook them in a little boiling salted water for about 5 minutes. Drain and place in a serving dish.

SLICE THE GARLIC VERY THINLY. Heat 1 tablespoon of olive oil in a pan, add the garlic and fry very briefly until it sizzles. Immediately add the remaining olive oil and vinegars to stop the cooking, and swirl together vigorously.

CHOP THE SUN-DRIED TOMATOES. Coarsely chop the capers. Swirl them into the dressing and season with pepper, adding a little salt only if needed. Pour the dressing over the salad.

SLICE THE OMELETTES into 5 mm ribbons and curl them loosely over the beans. Serve the salad accompanied by olive bread.

Sweet potato cakes with baked garlic

SERVES 4

450 g sweet potatoes
225 g potatoes
15 g fresh coriander roots
2 tbsp chopped fresh
   coriander leaves
50 g desiccated coconut,
   toasted
15 g plain flour, plus extra
   for dusting
1 tsp sesame oil
50 g sesame seeds
oil, for shallow-frying
salt and freshly ground pepper

For the baked garlic
2 heads of garlic, about
   125 g total weight
1 tbsp dark soy sauce
1 tbsp lemon juice
pinch of salt
pinch of sugar

For the chilli relish
2 garlic cloves
2–3 small green chillies,
   deseeded
1 tsp sea salt
1 tbsp rice wine vinegar
1 tbsp dark muscovado sugar
2 tbsp lemon juice

FIRST MAKE THE BAKED GARLIC. Preheat the oven to 200°C/Gas 6. Cut a small slice from the top of each garlic head and sit on a double layer of foil. Combine the soy sauce, lemon juice, salt and sugar in a bowl, then pour this mixture over the garlic. Seal the foil and bake for 30 minutes. Set aside until required.

TO MAKE THE CHILLI RELISH, roughly chop the garlic and chillies and grind to a smooth paste with the salt and dried shrimp using a spice grinder or a pestle and mortar. Transfer to a dish and stir in the remaining ingredients. Set aside.

FOR THE POTATO CAKES, peel and cube all the potatoes and place in a saucepan. Scrub and chop the coriander roots and add to the pan. Add enough cold water to cover, bring to the boil and cook for 12–15 minutes, until tender. Drain, return to the heat for a few seconds to dry out the potato, then mash until smooth. Allow to cool slightly.

STIR IN THE CHOPPED CORIANDER, the coconut, flour and sesame oil. Season with salt and pepper to taste. With lightly floured hands, form the mixture into 12 small patties. Dip the potato cakes in the sesame seeds to coat.

HEAT A SHALLOW LAYER OF OIL in a heavy-based, non-stick frying pan. Fry the potato cakes in batches for 2–3 minutes on each side until golden and heated through. Drain on kitchen paper.

SERVE THE POTATO CAKES HOT with the caramelised garlic cloves and a spoonful of chilli relish.

2

MAIN COURSES

Here you can find all the traditional Christmas favourites, plus lots of other ideas to ring the changes. There are tempting recipes for poultry, meat, fish and vegetarian dishes — something for everyone.

Turkey with lemon and sage butter and cranberry and orange stuffing

SERVES 8—10

Why mess with a good thing? This is as traditional as it gets. You can get everything ready the night before and then just cook it off on the day.

1 x 5 kg turkey (preferably free-range or sustainably raised)
2 lemons, zested and then cut in half
good bunch each of rosemary and thyme
olive oil

For the sage and lemon butter
bunch of sage, leaves picked and stalks reserved
250 g butter, at room temperature
2 lemons, zested and then cut in half
salt and freshly ground pepper

FIRST, MAKE SURE YOUR TURKEY is ready. Pull out any feather stubs that have been left in — a pair of tweezers makes this easier. Also, don't forget to check if there is a bag of giblets inside that needs to be taken out. They'll be pretty nasty if you cook them by mistake. Save them for the gravy.

NEXT, MAKE THE SAGE and lemon butter: chop through the sage leaves once, leaving them in fairly big pieces. Put these in a bowl with 250 g of the butter, half the lemon zest and a good bit of seasoning. Mix it all together.

NOW LOOSEN THE SKIN on the breast and legs of the turkey by carefully pushing your fingers under it; don't go mad, or you'll tear the skin and then it will shrink away from the breast as it cooks.

PUT THE SAGE BUTTER in a piping bag and push the nozzle under the skin on one side of the breast. Squeeze out some butter, then smooth it around, going down to where the leg meets the body. Repeat this on the other side of the breast.

NOW SEASON THE CAVITY of the bird. I know you don't eat the inside of the turkey, but seasoning well everywhere is critical for the final flavour.

[Continued overleaf]

For the stuffing

150 g caster sugar
1 tsp salt
150 g butter, at room
    temperature
300 g cranberries
2 lemons, zested and then
    cut in half
2 oranges, zested and then
    cut in half
4 cloves, roughly crushed
½ tsp cinnamon
350 g breadcrumbs

PUSH 4 LEMON HALVES, the reserved sage stalks and the rosemary and thyme into the bird. Rub the breast with olive oil (not butter, it will burn) and that's it. You can leave the turkey overnight in the fridge, but make sure you take it out a couple of hours before you want to cook it.

YOU CAN MAKE THE STUFFING ahead, or while the bird's cooking, as it will be cooked separately. Start off by heating a frying pan. Add the sugar and salt, and let the sugar start to caramelise, shaking the pan to keep the colour even. Once the sugar has melted and turned a golden colour, add half the butter and swirl it in. Now add the cranberries, the lemon and orange zests, the cloves and cinnamon. It's important to keep the mixture over a high heat so it keeps caramelising — bubble everything together to cook the cranberries, but don't turn them to sludge.

HEAT THE REMAINING BUTTER in another pan and let it brown slightly; you don't want it to brown too much, just enough to give a good nutty flavour. Add 1 tablespoon olive oil if it starts to get too brown. Tip in the breadcrumbs and stir to fry them a little, then add the juice from half a lemon and half an orange. Tip most of the breadcrumb mixture into a bowl (keep back a little). Now tip in the cranberry mixture and mix well. Add the reserved breadcrumbs if you need to. Set aside until cool enough to handle, then shape the mixture into balls or tip it into a buttered tin. Chill until you need it.

IF YOU'RE DOING ROAST POTATOES, you can parboil them ahead, and you can also make the stock for the gravy (see opposite).

Giblet gravy

The stock for the gravy can be made the day before it's needed. Heat a little oil in a pan and fry the giblets until they are browned all over. Add 600 ml water and stir, then add 3 chopped shallots, 2 bay leaves, a few thyme sprigs and 6 black peppercorns. Bring to a boil and skim. Turn down the heat and simmer for 1 hour. Strain and set aside.

On Christmas Day the gravy can be made while the stuffing is cooking. Pour away the fat from the roasting tin without losing the turkey juices. Place over a medium heat and stir in 1 tablespoon flour. Cook for 2 minutes, then whisk in 100 ml red wine, followed by the stock. Simmer for 15 minutes and season.

ON CHRISTMAS DAY calculate what time you need to put the turkey in (15 minutes to start it off and then 30 minutes per kg). Preheat the oven to 220°C/Gas 7.

DRIZZLE A BIT MORE OIL on the turkey and roast it for 15 minutes. Turn the oven down to 180°C/Gas 4, cover the bird with foil and roast for 2½ hours, or until the juices run clear when you pierce the thigh with a skewer. Take the turkey out, cover with foil and a tea towel and leave to rest. Meanwhile, put the stuffing in the oven and cook for 30 minutes, or until it's brown on the outside and heated through. Carve the turkey nicely with a sharp knife.

Roast duck with cider sauce

SERVES 3

Apples and duck are a traditional pairing, the sharpness of the fruit providing a contrast to the richness of the meat. In this recipe, cider does the job of the apples, and very good it is too. If you wish, apple sauce could also be served with the bird.

1 x 1.8 kg oven-ready duck
300 ml cider
1 tbsp cider vinegar
1 tbsp plain flour
salt and freshly ground pepper

PREHEAT THE OVEN to 200°C/Gas 6.

Weigh the duck and calculate the cooking time at 20 minutes per 450 g (a 1.8 kg bird will take about 1½ hours).

PRICK THE SKIN ALL OVER. Season the duck cavity with salt and pepper, and rub salt all over the outside. Put the bird breast-side down on a rack in a roasting tin and place in the oven for 30 minutes. Pour off the fat, turn the bird over and continue roasting for about another hour. When it's cooked, the juices should run pale pink when the thigh is pierced with a skewer.

POUR THE CAVITY JUICES into a bowl. Transfer the duck to a warmed serving plate and keep warm without covering so that the skin remains crisp.

TO MAKE THE SAUCE, pour off all but 1 tablespoon of the fat from the roasting tin. Add the flour and mix well, scraping up the sediment. Stir in the reserved cavity juices, the cider and vinegar, stirring until smooth. Simmer for a few minutes, then taste and add seasoning. Strain and serve with the duck.

Duck confit and sauté potatoes

SERVES 8

A canard gras is a duck that has been reared for foie gras. It will weigh about 6 kg and may seem expensive, but inside it has a whole foie gras. If you cannot find such a duck, I suggest using eight large duck legs or two ordinary ducks.

1 canard gras
1 kg good-quality coarse sea salt
1 sage sprig
1 thyme sprig

For the sauté potatoes
1 kg potatoes (Amandine or similar), boiled in their skin and cooled
3 garlic cloves, chopped
1 bunch flatleaf parsley, chopped
salt and freshly ground pepper

IF USING A CANARD GRAS, remove the legs and breasts, trim off any excess fat and discard the head. Add the neck skin to the fat and the neck to the meat.

TAKE OUT THE FOIE GRAS, wrap in clingfilm and refrigerate to use for another recipe. Wash the heart and gizzard, cut in half and add to the meat.

TRIM ALL THE SKIN AND FAT off the carcass. Put all the fat in a pan and cover with water. Bring to a gentle simmer to render – about 1 hour. Pour the fat through a fine conical sieve without pressing.

LIBERALLY SPRINKLE THE MEAT with the sea salt and chill for 90 minutes. Wipe with a cloth, then put the meat into the warm fat with the sage and thyme. Bring to a gentle simmer, cover with grease proof paper and cook for about 2 hours, until tender.

ALLOW THE WHOLE DISH TO COOL, then store in an airtight container. It will keep for several weeks.

TO USE THE DUCK CONFIT, preheat the oven to 180°C/Gas 4. Place the meat in a non-stick pan and cook over a medium heat until golden. Transfer to the hot oven for 10–15 minutes.

NOW MAKE THE SAUTÉ POTATOES. Peel the potatoes when cool. Cut into 5 mm slices and pan-fry in 3 tablespoons of the duck fat. Season and sprinkle with garlic and parsley.

Duck with orange, cranberry and thyme

SERVES 6

Duck is a popular choice for entertaining, and this delicious dish takes advantage of the cheaper leg cut. It's made very attractive by the cranberries in the sauce, and, once garnished with watercress, looks very professional. Serve with roast potatoes and a selection of seasonal vegetables.

SEASON THE DUCK LEGS and fry 3 of them in a dry frying pan over a high heat for 5 minutes. Drain on kitchen paper and transfer to a casserole, then do the same with the remaining 3 legs.

PREHEAT THE OVEN to 180°C/Gas 4.

IN A SMALL BOWL, mix the cornflour and orange juice to a paste and set aside.

IN A SEPARATE BOWL, mix together the orange rind, cranberries, chicken stock, thyme, shallots, sherry, turnips and seasoning and spoon over the duck. Stir in the cornflour paste. Place in the oven and cook for 1 hour.

SERVE THE DUCK garnished with watercress.

6 duck legs, skin on
2 tbsp cornflour
150 ml orange juice
rind pared in a single piece
　　from 1 orange
75 g dried cranberries
300 ml chicken stock
2 tbsp chopped thyme
400 g shallots
250 ml fino sherry
200 g small turnips, quartered
salt and freshly ground pepper
80 g watercress, to garnish

Guinea fowl with baby turnips and salsa verde

SERVES 4

This recipe is inspired by bollito misto, an elaborate dish from the Piedmont region of Italy.

1 whole guinea fowl
2 bay leaves
3 fresh flatleaf parsley sprigs
3 large fresh thyme sprigs
1 lemon, halved
150 ml dry white wine
200 g baby turnips, peeled
200 g baby carrots, trimmed
  and scrubbed
200 g new potatoes,
  peeled and halved
salt and freshly ground pepper

For the salsa verde
1 garlic clove, finely chopped
2 anchovy fillets in olive oil,
  drained and finely chopped
1 tbsp salted or brined capers,
  rinsed and finely chopped
3 tbsp roughly chopped fresh
  flatleaf parsley
3 tbsp roughly chopped
  fresh mint
1 tbsp red wine vinegar
3 tbsp extra virgin olive oil

SEASON THE GUINEA FOWL inside and out, then push the herbs and lemon into the body cavity. Sit the guinea fowl breast-side down on a double piece of foil large enough to enclose it loosely, then lift the foil up and around it, leaving an opening at the top. Pour the wine into this opening, then scrunch the foil closed into a loose package.

BRING THE WATER in your steamer to the boil. Place the guinea fowl in the steamer and steam, covered, over a gentle simmer, for 1 hour, regularly checking the water level and adding more if necessary.

MEANWHILE, combine all the ingredients for the salsa verde in a bowl and set aside.

WHEN THE GUINEA FOWL is cooked through, remove it from the steamer and let it sit in its foil wrapping for 15 minutes.

TOP UP THE WATER in your steamer and bring it to a rolling boil. Add the turnips, carrots and potatoes, season well and steam, covered, for 10 minutes, until just tender.

SKIN THE GUINEA FOWL and carve it onto a serving plate. Surround with the steamed vegetables and spoon the bird's cooking juices over the whole dish. Serve with the salsa verde on the side.

Roast pheasant with grapes and nuts

SERVES 6

In this recipe, tender pheasants are glazed with clementine juice, crushed grapes and Madeira and roasted to perfection. The liquids in the pan stop the pheasant drying out, especially if you baste during cooking. The pan juices are then used to make a rich sauce that's Russian in inspiration.

6 clementines
700 g white or red grapes
40 fresh walnuts in shell,
    or 225 g walnut halves
1 tbsp green tea
200 ml Madeira or sweet sherry
2 young pheasants, plucked,
    drawn and trussed, with
    giblets.
softened butter, for basting
2 tsp balsamic or sherry vinegar
1 tbsp dark soy sauce
salt and freshly ground pepper

To garnish
extra grapes
pheasant feathers, if available

PREHEAT THE OVEN to 200°C/Gas 6.

GRATE THE RIND from 2 clementines and squeeze the juice from all 6; place in a bowl. Reserve the ungrated squeezed halves. Whizz the grapes roughly in a food processor and pour into the clementine juice. Shell the fresh walnuts (if using). Pour 300 ml boiling water over the tea, leave for 5 minutes, then strain and reserve.

POUR HALF the clementine and grape juice into a roasting tin, adding the Madeira and any giblets (except the liver). Place the reserved clementine halves inside the pheasant cavities. Smear the pheasants with butter and season with salt and pepper.

PLACE THE BIRDS in the roasting tin on one side, leg uppermost. Roast in the oven for 15 minutes. Turn the birds over on the other side, baste with the pan juices and roast for another 15 minutes. Finally, sit the birds upright, baste well and roast for a final 15 minutes, or until done. Test by pushing a skewer into the meatiest part of the thigh: the juices should run clear. Transfer the birds to a warmed serving platter and keep warm.

POUR THE RESERVED clementine and grape juice into the roasting tin. Stir in the tea, vinegar and soy sauce. Place over the heat and bring to the boil, scraping up any sediment from the bottom of the pan. Boil for 1–2 minutes, then strain into a saucepan, pressing the juice through the sieve with the back of a wooden spoon. Stir in the walnuts, bring to the boil and reduce to 450 ml. Taste and season well. The sauce should be slightly syrupy: if not, reduce a little more. Spoon the walnuts around the pheasant and pour the sauce into a warmed sauceboat. Serve straight away.

JAMES MARTIN

Roasted partridge with creamed sprouts and chestnuts

SERVES 4

Hate Brussels sprouts? Try these and you'll be converted. The partridge is pretty good too!

4 partridges, cleaned and
    halved lengthways
1 tbsp olive oil
25 g butter
salt and freshly ground pepper

For the sprouts
50 g butter
1 tbsp olive oil
2 shallots, finely sliced
300 g Brussels sprouts,
    trimmed and finely sliced
2 thyme sprigs
110 ml white wine
200 ml double cream
150 g cooked chestnuts,
    roughly chopped
3 tbsp chopped fresh
    flatleaf parsley

For the sauce
75 g butter
1 shallot, finely chopped
75 ml red wine
175 ml chicken stock

PREHEAT THE OVEN to 220°C/Gas 7.

SEASON THE PARTRIDGES with salt and black pepper. Heat a frying pan, add the olive oil and butter, then put the partridges in it skin-side down. Cook for 1–2 minutes on each side, until golden, then transfer to a roasting tin and place in the oven for 12–15 minutes. Remove and set aside to rest.

WHILE THE PARTRIDGES ARE RESTING, prepare the sprouts. Heat the butter and oil in a frying pan. Add the shallots and fry for 1–2 minutes, then add the sprouts and stir-fry for 1 minute. Add the thyme and white wine and bring to a simmer. Cook for 2 minutes, then add the cream and cook for a further 2 minutes. Add the chestnuts, season with salt and pepper, and stir in the parsley.

TO MAKE THE SAUCE, heat a second frying pan, add half the butter and the shallot and sauté for 2 minutes. Add the wine and bring to the boil, then lower the heat and cook until reduced by half. Add the chicken stock and bring back to the boil. Simmer for 3 minutes, until the sauce has reduced and thickened slightly. Season with salt and pepper, then whisk in the rest of the butter.

TO SERVE, pile the sprouts in the centre of your serving plates and top each one with 2 halves of partridge. Spoon the red wine sauce around the edge.

Goose breast with seasonal vegetables

SERVES 2

I devised this dish for Barbara Windsor when she came on *Ready, Steady, Cook* for a festive celebrity special. I called it 'Goosie Gander Windsor'.

1 goose breast, trimmed (skin on)
2 x 225 g potatoes, cut into 8 wedges
1 large parsnip, diced
175 ml red wine
120 ml chicken stock
grated rind of 1 orange
pinch of ground mixed spice
50 g chilled unsalted butter, diced
8 large Brussels sprouts, trimmed and grated
1 garlic clove, crushed
120 ml double cream
1 tbsp fresh thyme leaves
salt and freshly ground pepper

PREHEAT THE OVEN to 200°C/Gas 6. Heat an ovenproof frying pan. Score the skin of the goose breast, then fry, skin-side down, until lightly golden. Cook on the other side for 1–2 minutes. Transfer to a wire rack set over the pan and roast for 10–15 minutes, or until the goose is tender and cooked through.

COOK THE POTATOES in boiling salted water for 6–8 minutes, until just tender. Boil the parsnip in another pan of salted water for 10–12 minutes, until tender.

PLACE THE WINE in another pan with the chicken stock, orange rind and mixed spice and boil fast until reduced by half. Heat half the butter in a small wok and add the Brussels sprouts and garlic. Stir-fry for 2–3 minutes, until just tender, then stir in half the cream and warm through. Season to taste.

HEAT A LARGE FRYING PAN and drain the potatoes. Drain the goose fat into the frying pan. Leave the breast in a warm place to rest for at least 5 minutes. Add the thyme to the pan, then the potatoes and cook for 3–4 minutes on each side, until lightly golden. Season.

DRAIN THE PARSNIPS and whizz in a food processor with the remaining cream. Season to taste.

CARVE THE GOOSE BREAST and put on warmed plates. Add the potatoes, plus dollops of parsnip purée and creamed sprouts. Whisk the remaining butter into the reduced wine mixture to warm through, then drizzle the sauce around the plates to serve.

Chicken with beans, hazelnuts and orange

SERVES 6

With crunchy hazelnuts, tangy oranges and succulent green beans, there's lots of texture and flavour in this tasty dish.

1.5 kg chicken thighs or
    drumsticks, skin removed
2 tbsp olive oil
6 shallots, roughly sliced
3 garlic cloves, chopped
1 tbsp plain flour
50 g hazelnuts, halved
100 ml hot chicken stock
100 ml fresh orange juice
200 g green beans, halved
4 tbsp chopped flatleaf parsley
1 kg new potatoes, to serve
salt and freshly ground pepper

PREHEAT THE OVEN to 180°C/Gas 4.

SEASON THE CHICKEN. Heat half the oil in a large frying pan over a medium heat and fry the chicken until golden all over. Transfer to a large ovenproof dish.

HEAT THE REMAINING OIL in the frying pan and soften the shallots and garlic. Stir in the flour, mixing well to remove any lumps. Add the hazelnuts, stock and orange juice and bring to the boil. Pour over the chicken, then cover the dish with foil and cook for about 45 minutes.

ABOUT 10 MINUTES before the end of the cooking time, add the beans and parsley.

MEANWHILE, cook the new potatoes over a high heat in a pan of lightly salted boiling water for 20 minutes, or until tender. Serve immediately with the chicken and sauce.

French roast chicken

SERVES 4

Roasting chicken the French way ensures that it is deliciously moist and tender, so it's worth the little extra effort involved. Don't be put off by the amount of garlic — it cooks down to a sweet-tasting, delicate purée that gives real body to the gravy. The gravy does require giblets, so search out a good free-range chicken; failing that, make do with ready-made chicken or vegetable stock.

1 x 1.4 kg roasting chicken, with giblets
1 carrot
1 onion
1 bouquet garni (1 bay leaf tied together with a sprig of rosemary and thyme)
140 g butter
2 fresh tarragon sprigs
½ lemon
6 garlic cloves
salt and freshly ground pepper
2 tsp plain flour

PREHEAT THE OVEN to 200°C/Gas 6.

REMOVE THE GIBLETS FROM THE CHICKEN and put them in a saucepan with the carrot, onion, bouquet garni and 600 ml water. Bring to the boil, then cover and simmer for 1 hour while the chicken is cooking.

WEIGH THE CHICKEN and calculate the cooking time, allowing 20 minutes per 450 g, plus 20 minutes. Melt 125 g of the butter. Put the tarragon and lemon inside the chicken. Lay the bird on its side on a rack in a roasting tin. Brush the uppermost side with butter. Roast in the oven for 20 minutes, then turn the bird so that the other side is uppermost. Brush with more butter and roast for a further 20 minutes.

TURN THE CHICKEN AGAIN so that the breast is uppermost. Brush with more butter. Scatter the garlic cloves in the base of the roasting tin. Cook the chicken for the remainder of the cooking time, or until the juices run clear when a thigh is pierced with a skewer. Transfer the chicken to a heated serving dish and leave to rest in a warm place for 10 minutes.

TO MAKE THE GRAVY, skim off excess fat from the roasting tin. Retrieve the garlic cloves and pop them out of their skins back into the tin; mash with a fork. Strain the giblet stock into the pan and bring to the boil.

BEAT TOGETHER the remaining butter and the flour. Whisk this beurre manié, a small piece at a time, into the gravy. Simmer for a few minutes, whisking all the time. Season to taste. Serve the chicken accompanied by the gravy and vegetables of your choice.

Beef fillet with a walnut crust

SERVES 6

Fillet of beef may seem a bit extravagant, but it is so deliciously rich, you don't need much — especially if you serve it with lots of vegetables. The piece of fillet is cut into thick steaks, which are topped with a savoury mixture of walnuts and anchovies, and popped into the oven at the last moment. A very easy dish — all prepared in advance.

350 g walnut pieces
125 g pickled walnuts, drained
1 x 50 g tin anchovies, drained
2 garlic cloves
1 tbsp thick soy sauce
3 tbsp olive oil
1–1.1 kg piece fillet of beef, trimmed
2 tbsp sunflower or corn oil
4 tbsp white wine
300 ml well-flavoured beef stock
salt and freshly ground pepper

To serve
4 large radicchio leaves (optional)
4 tbsp chopped fresh parsley
parsley sprigs, to garnish

ROUGHLY CHOP both types of walnut together. Set aside half of the mixture. Place the other half in a blender or food processor with the anchovies, garlic, soy sauce and olive oil. Blend until smooth. Stir in the reserved walnuts and season with salt and pepper; the paste should be quite thick and lumpy.

WITH A SHARP KNIFE, slice the fillet into 6 thick steaks. Heat the oil in a heavy-based frying pan until almost smoking. Fry the steaks, one at a time, very quickly on all sides to brown and seal. Allow to cool. Top each steak thickly with the anchovy and walnut paste. Cover and refrigerate until you're ready to cook them.

TO MAKE THE GRAVY, deglaze the frying pan with the wine, stirring to scrape up the sediment. Add the beef stock, bring to the boil and boil steadily for 2–3 minutes until reduced slightly. Check the seasoning. Pour into a bowl and cool. Cover and refrigerate until needed.

REMOVE THE STEAKS from the refrigerator 15–20 minutes before cooking to allow them to come to room temperature.

PREHEAT THE OVEN to 200°C/Gas 6.

PLACE THE STEAKS on a baking sheet. Bake in the oven for 10–15 minutes, depending on thickness and preference for rare or medium steaks. Meanwhile, reheat the gravy in a small pan.

SERVE THE STEAKS on warmed plates as soon as they are cooked. If desired, place each one on a radicchio leaf. Sprinkle with plenty of chopped parsley and garnish with extra parsley sprigs. Serve with the gravy.

Grilled rib of beef

SERVES 4

There's no secret to a good rib of beef: to me it's obvious that if you buy beef from a small farm (not necessarily organic) that takes care of its animals and feeds and breeds them properly, you have a good chance of enjoying a fine piece of beef. The meat should be well hung — four weeks in my view.

2 ribs of beef, about 350 g each
olive oil
salt and freshly ground
   black pepper

RUB THE TRIMMED RIBS with a little olive oil, salt and pepper.

SET THE MEAT on the grill over a medium heat. This is a thick cut of meat, so it needs to cook slowly. Turn so that it cooks and marks evenly. It should take 20 minutes for medium rare.

DON'T FORGET to let it rest at least 10 minutes in a warm place before carving.

ANGELA HARTNETT

Rib-eye steaks with tomatoes and olives

SERVES 4

In the UK we don't tend to associate olives with beef, but they give it a fantastic saltiness. This recipe is like an Italian version of classic British steak with roast tomatoes. You don't have to use rib-eye; thin slices of rump or fillet will do just as well.

1 tbsp butter
2 tbsp olive oil
4 x 200 g rib-eye steaks
4 plum tomatoes, seeded and quartered
10 black olives, pitted and coarsely chopped
10 caperberries, cut in half
salt and freshly ground pepper

For the vinaigrette
20 ml good red wine vinegar
100 ml olive oil
salt

HEAT THE BUTTER and olive oil in a heavy-based frying pan over a fairly high heat until bubbling. Season the steaks and add to the pan. Cook for 4–6 minutes, turning halfway through, depending on whether you prefer your steak rare or medium. Transfer to a plate and set aside to rest for a few minutes.

NOW MAKE THE VINAIGRETTE. Put the vinegar in a bowl, season well and mix until the salt is completely dissolved. Add the olive oil and whisk together.

DRAIN THE EXCESS OIL from the pan and add the tomatoes, olives and caperberries. Cook lightly, stirring, for 1 minute, then add to the vinaigrette.

CUT THE STEAKS on the diagonal into equal pieces and serve with the vinaigrette drizzled over the top. Serve with sautéd potatoes.

Tournedos with 'caponata' and Pineau des Charentes sauce

1 beef tournedos per person
  (about 200 g each)
clarified butter, for frying
salt and freshly ground pepper

For the anchovy butter (serves 10)
15 g shallots, chopped
30 ml white wine
20 g anchovy fillets in oil, drained
125 g soft butter
5 g chopped parsley
lemon juice, to taste

For the sauce (serves 10)
2 shallots, sliced
vegetable oil, for frying
100 ml Chardonnay vinegar
275 ml white Pineau des
  Charentes liqueur
1 litre beef stock
butter

For the caponata (serves 1)
12 aubergine batons, 2 cm long
12 red onion batons, 2 cm long
12 courgette batons, 2 cm long
4 yellow pepper batons, 2 cm long
4 red pepper batons, 2 cm long
olive oil, for frying
6 small batons black olives
10 pine kernels, toasted
10 sultanas
5 halves sun-dried tomatoes,
  diced
8 cooked chickpeas

FIRST MAKE THE ANCHOVY BUTTER. Cook the shallots and wine until soft. Cool and drain.

CHOP THE ANCHOVIES to a fine paste and mix into the butter. Add the parsley and cooled shallots, then season with pepper and lemon juice. Roll the anchovy butter into a log, wrap in clingfilm and chill until set.

NOW MAKE THE SAUCE. Put the shallots and a little oil in a saucepan and cook until caramelised. Deglaze the pan with the vinegar, then reduce by three-quarters.

ADD THE PINEAU and beef stock, then bring to the boil. Simmer very slowly for 45 minutes, skimming now and then. Pass the sauce through a fine chinois, then reduce until it coats the back of a spoon. Set aside.

TO MAKE THE CAPONATA, sweat the aubergine, onion, courgette and pepper batons with a splash of olive oil until cooked but not too soft. Add the remaining ingredients and season with salt and pepper. Cook gently for a few minutes and keep warm.

SEASON THE TOURNEDOS with salt and pan-fry in hot clarified butter — about 12 minutes for rare and 16 minutes for medium. When cooked, season the meat with pepper and leave to rest for 5 minutes.

TO SERVE, bring the sauce back to the boil and add a knob of butter, a pinch of salt and a splash of Pineau. Place the caponata in the centre of a plate and sit one tournedos on it. Top with a slice of anchovy butter, pour the sauce around the caponata and enjoy.

MICHEL ROUX JR

Leg of venison with lemon and honey

SERVES 8

Michel says, 'I love game at Christmas, especially venison. The long, slow cooking with lemon and honey fills the house with a fragrant, tummy-rumbling smell. With such powerful flavours, I serve a rich red wine, such as an Australian shiraz.'

1 x 3 kg leg of venison
olive oil
juice of 1 lemon
4 tbsp clear honey
4 onions, coarsely sliced
1 large or 2 small lemons,
    cut into wedges
1 thyme sprig
generous glass white wine
salt and freshly ground pepper

RUB THE VENISON LEG with a little olive oil, salt, pepper, lemon juice and 1 tablespoon of honey. Cover with clingfilm, place in the fridge and leave to marinate overnight.

PREHEAT THE OVEN to 220°C/Gas 7.

WARM A LARGE ROASTING TRAY on top of the stove and sear the venison with a good bit of olive oil. Once the meat is coloured on all sides, put it in the hot oven for 10 minutes.

REMOVE FROM THE OVEN and add the sliced onions, lemon wedges, 3 tablespoon of honey, the thyme and wine. Reduce the heat to 180°C/Gas 4 and return the meat to the oven for 30 minutes. Turn off the oven and leave the venison inside for a further 30 minutes. Take to the table to carve.

Venison casserole with red wine and spices

SERVES 6—8

Venison steaks are ideal for marinating in wine with spices, and then casseroling to a moist tenderness. Lighten the richness with plenty of vegetables. Creamed potatoes and sautéd cabbage are ideal accompaniments.

900 g lean venison chunks
2 tbsp plain flour
2 tbsp oil
225 g baby onions
125 g rindless streaky bacon, diced
½ small celeriac, cut into chunks
300 ml beef stock
1 cinnamon stick, halved
225 g wild mushrooms
1 tbsp wine vinegar
1 tbsp redcurrant jelly
salt and freshly ground pepper
bay leaves, to garnish

For the marinade
1 large onion, quartered
2 carrots, roughly chopped
3 garlic cloves
2 fresh bay leaves
4—6 whole cloves
1 tbsp allspice
4 tbsp brandy
300 ml red wine

PLACE THE VENISON in a large bowl. Add the marinade ingredients, stir well, then cover and leave in the refrigerator for 2—3 days, turning daily.

PREHEAT THE OVEN to 160°C/Gas 3.

THOROUGHLY DRAIN THE VENISON, reserving the marinade. Pat the meat dry on kitchen paper. Season the flour with salt and pepper and use to coat the meat.

HEAT THE OIL in a flameproof casserole, add the venison and sear on all sides. Remove with a slotted spoon. Add the onions and bacon to the casserole and fry for 3 minutes. Return the venison to the pan with the celeriac. Strain the marinade juices over the meat, then add the stock and cinnamon stick. Bring just to the boil, lower the heat and cover with a tight-fitting lid. Cook in the oven for 1 hour. Add the mushrooms, wine vinegar and redcurrant jelly to the casserole, then return to the oven for a further hour.

LADLE THE STEW onto warmed serving plates and garnish with the bay leaves.

Orange and rosemary glazed rack of lamb

SERVES 4—6

2 racks of lamb (about 7 chops
    in each), chine bone removed
    and French-trimmed
4 tbsp Mary Berry's
    All Seasons Sauce
1 fresh rosemary sprig
2 garlic cloves, cut in half
2 oranges, segmented for
    garnish (save any juice)

PUT THE RACKS OF LAMB into a polythene bag with the All Seaons Sauce, fresh rosemary (sprig kept whole) and pieces of garlic. Massage the sauce into the lamb and leave to marinate in the fridge for as long as possible.

PREHEAT THE OVEN to 200°C/Gas 6.

REMOVE THE RACKS from the marinade and arrange in a small roasting tin. Roast in the oven for about 15—20 minutes, until just cooked but pink in the middle.

DISCARD THE ROSEMARY AND GARLIC from the marinade and heat the remaining liquid in a pan, adding any spare juice from the oranges.

CARVE BETWEEN THE CHOPS, serve with the sauce and garnish with the orange segments.

Roast lamb with garlic and mushroom stuffing

SERVES 8

As with most great British roasts, lamb is traditionally cooked with little embellishment to allow the flavour of the meat to dominate. To impart extra flavour, a robust garlic, mushroom and leek stuffing is included here. To save yourself time, order a boned leg of lamb from the butcher several days in advance and use the bone to make the stock for the gravy.

225 g brown mushrooms
6 large garlic cloves
1 leek
4 tbsp olive oil
3 tbsp chopped fresh oregano
1 x 2.3 kg boned leg of lamb
3–4 tbsp redcurrant jelly
2 tsp red wine vinegar
150 ml red wine
300 ml lamb stock
salt and freshly ground pepper
herb sprigs, to garnish

WIPE THE MUSHROOMS and peel the garlic. Place both in a food processor and work briefly until finely chopped. Trim and chop the leek. Heat the oil in a frying pan. Add the mushrooms, garlic and leek and fry for about 10 minutes until the mushroom juices have evaporated and the mixture has the consistency of a thick paste. Stir in the oregano and season with salt and pepper. Leave to cool.

PREHEAT THE OVEN to 180°C/Gas 4. Open out the lamb and pack the stuffing down the centre. Fold the meat over the stuffing to enclose it and tie with string. Place the lamb seam-side down in a roasting tin.

ROAST THE LAMB for 25 minutes per 450 g plus 25 minutes for medium; 30 minutes per 450 g plus 30 minutes for well done.

MELT THE REDCURRANT JELLY in a small saucepan with the wine vinegar. Thirty minutes before the end of the roasting time, brush the lamb with the redcurrant glaze. Repeat several times before the end of the cooking time.

REMOVE THE LAMB from the tin and transfer to a warmed serving platter. Keep warm. Drain off the fat from the pan and stir in the wine and stock. Bring to the boil and boil until slightly reduced. Strain the gravy, if preferred, into a warmed sauceboat.

REMOVE THE STRING from the lamb. Surround with the sprigs of herbs and serve accompanied by the gravy and vegetables of your choice.

Lamb shanks with orange, bay and juniper berries

SERVES 4

A comforting and warming dish of melt-in-the-mouth lamb flavoured with the earthy perfume of juniper berries.

4 lamb shanks
grated rind and juice of
½ orange
1 tbsp grainy mustard
1 tbsp redcurrant jelly
4 bay leaves
1 tbsp juniper berries,
roughly crushed
salt and freshly ground pepper
freshly steamed rice or couscous
or potato mash, to serve

PREPARE A LARGE STEAMER and bring the water in it to the boil.

PLACE EACH LAMB SHANK on a double thickness of foil large enough to encase it completely. Combine the orange rind and juice, mustard and jelly, add ½ teaspoon salt and a good grinding of black pepper. Rub this mixture all over the lamb shanks. Divide the bay leaves and juniper berries between the 4 pieces of foil. Lift the foil, scrunching it together to loosely enclose each shank.

PLACE THE LAMB SHANK PARCELS on the perforated shelf of your steamer, cover with a lid and steam over a very low heat for 1¾ hours, regularly checking the water level and adding more if necessary.

REMOVE THE PARCELS from the steamer and leave to stand for 10 minutes before unwrapping. Serve with rice, couscous or mashed potato to soak up the juices.

Moroccan lamb with lemons and olives

SERVES 6

Here's a North African speciality with an intense lemony flavour. Adjust the strength of the flavour once the casserole is cooked – it will depend on the size of your lemons and the freshness of your spices (stale ones will not give the same depth of flavour).

1 x 1.4 kg boned leg or
   shoulder of lamb
2 large onions
3 large lemons
3 tbsp olive oil
1 large bunch of flatleaf parsley
225 g green olives
salt and freshly ground pepper
1 red onion, to garnish

For the Moroccan spice mixture
3 tbsp ground ginger
3 tbsp ground turmeric
3 tbsp coarsely ground
   black pepper
3 tbsp ground cinnamon
1 tbsp ground nutmeg
1 tbsp hot curry powder

FIRST MAKE THE SPICE MIXTURE. Put all the spices in a small bowl and mix together thoroughly. Transfer to an airtight container and use as required. Store for up to a month.

TRIM THE LAMB of any excess fat and cut into 5 cm cubes. Roughly chop the onions.

PARE A STRIP OF RIND from 1 lemon. Cut into shreds and set aside for the garnish.

HEAT THE OIL in a flameproof casserole. Add the onions and cook over a fairly high heat for 2 minutes; remove from the pan. Quickly fry the meat in batches over a very high heat until nicely browned all over. Return all the meat and the onions to the casserole.

ADD 3 TABLESPOONS of the spice mixture and cook, stirring all the time, for 2 minutes. Add 150 ml water and the juice of the pared lemon. Bring to the boil, then lower the heat. Cover with a lid and cook gently for 1–1½ hours, or until the lamb is really tender.

MEANWHILE, finely chop the parsley. Finely grate the rind from the two remaining lemons.

ADD THE OLIVES to the casserole with the grated lemon rind and half the parsley. Season with salt and pepper. Add a little more water if the liquid has completely reduced, but not too much – it should be fairly thick. Cook for a further 10 minutes.

CHOP THE RED ONION. Taste and adjust the flavour of the casserole, adding more lemon juice if necessary. Serve sprinkled with the remaining parsley, red onion and shredded lemon rind.

Smoked pork loin with saupiquet sauce

SERVES 4

Here thick slices of boiled or baked smoked pork loin are served with a piquant cream and mustard sauce, scented with peppercorns and juniper berries. Serve with a green vegetable, such as cabbage or French beans, and boiled or creamy mashed potatoes.

1 x 700 g boneless smoked
    pork loin roast
chopped parsley, to garnish

For the sauce
4 shallots
50 g butter
25 g plain flour
300 ml dry white wine
300 ml light meat or
    vegetable stock
4 juniper berries, crushed
1 tsp mixed dried peppercorns,
    crushed
50 ml white wine vinegar
1 tbsp Dijon mustard
100 ml crème fraîche or double
    cream
salt and freshly ground pepper

THE PORK LOIN can be boiled or baked. To boil, place in a saucepan, cover with water and bring to the boil. Lower the heat and simmer for 20 minutes per 450 g plus 20 minutes. To bake, place in a roasting tin in an oven preheated to 160°C/Gas 3 for 45 minutes per 450 g plus 15 minutes.

MEANWHILE, peel and chop the shallots. Melt the butter in a saucepan, add the flour and cook, stirring, for about 3 minutes, until foaming. Gradually whisk in the wine and stock, then add the juniper berries and half the shallots. Bring to the boil, stirring, and simmer for 10 minutes.

PLACE THE MIXED PEPPERCORNS, remaining shallots and vinegar in a saucepan and boil to reduce the liquid to 2 teaspoonfuls. Dip the base of the pan into cold water to prevent further reduction. Pour the wine sauce into the reduced vinegar and stir in the mustard. Bring to the boil, lower the heat and simmer for 15–20 minutes, until the shallots are cooked. Stir in the crème fraîche and bring to the boil. Check the seasoning.

TO SERVE, carve the pork loin into thick slices and arrange in a warmed serving dish. Spoon the sauce over the meat and serve at once, garnished with the chopped parsley.

Pork with a Calvados, apple and sage stuffing

SERVES 4

This traditional French flavour combination is given a contemporary, healthy steamed treatment in this recipe.

4 pieces of pork fillet (about 175 g each)
1 Granny Smith apple, coarsely grated

For the stuffing
2 tsp olive oil
1 small onion, finely chopped
6 fresh sage leaves, finely chopped
2 garlic cloves, crushed
3 tbsp Calvados
salt and freshly ground pepper

FIRST MAKE THE STUFFING. Heat the oil in a pan over a low heat. Add the onion and sage and sauté for 8–10 minutes, until the onion is soft and translucent. Add the garlic and cook for 1 further minute. Increase the heat to high, pour in the Calvados and continue to cook, stirring, for 1 minute. Remove the pan from the heat and let the stuffing cool to room temperature.

USING A SMALL SHARP KNIFE, slice a horizontal opening in the thickest part of each pork fillet. Stir the grated apple into the cooled stuffing mixture and season with salt and pepper. Stuff half the mixture into the pockets of the pork fillets. Season the outside of the fillets with salt and pepper, then place in a shallow heatproof dish that will fit in your steamer. Top with the remaining apple, sage and onion mixture and cover the dish with foil.

BRING THE WATER IN YOUR STEAMER to a gentle simmer. Place the dish in the steamer, cover with a lid and steam over a low heat for 18–20 minutes, until it is just cooked through. You don't want to serve the meat pink, but make sure you don't overcook it, otherwise the fibres will toughen and need about 45 minutes' steaming to become tender again.

Glazed pork loin with fig stuffing

SERVES 6

It is important to score the crackling deeply to ensure a crisp result. The crackling bastes the meat during cooking and keeps it moist.

1 x 1.4 kg boned loin of pork, skin well scored
salt and freshly ground pepper

For the fig stuffing
4 shallots
1 garlic clove
225 g no-need-to-soak dried figs
1 eating apple
2 fresh rosemary sprigs
50 g butter
finely grated rind and juice of 1 lemon
3 tbsp dry sherry

For the glaze
4 tbsp clear honey
2 tsp mustard powder
finely grated rind of 1 lemon

To garnish
rosemary sprigs
4 or 5 fresh figs

FIRST MAKE THE STUFFING. Peel and finely chop the shallots. Crush the garlic. Roughly chop the dried figs. Peel, core and finely chop the apple. Chop the rosemary.

MELT THE BUTTER in a saucepan and add the shallots and garlic. Cook for 5–10 minutes, until soft and golden. Stir in the figs, apple, rosemary, lemon rind and juice, and sherry. Cook, stirring, for 5 minutes, until slightly softened and most of the liquid has evaporated. Leave to cool.

PREHEAT THE OVEN to 190°C/Gas 5. Open out the pork loin and lay skin-side down on a clean surface. Season well with salt and pepper and spread the stuffing along the middle. Roll up and tie at intervals with fine string. Place in a roasting tin and roast in the oven for 1 hour.

MEANWHILE, make the glaze. Place the honey, mustard and lemon rind in a saucepan and heat gently, stirring. Brush over the pork skin and roast for a further 45 minutes, basting every 15 minutes with the glaze.

LEAVE THE MEAT TO REST in a warm place for 15 minutes. Carve into thick slices and serve garnished with sprigs of rosemary and the fresh figs. Accompany with a gravy made from the pan juices if wished, and seasonal vegetables.

Cheese and ham pie

SERVES 6–8 AS A MAIN COURSE

This is great as a main course or as a starter. It is best warm, but also very tasty served cold from the fridge. Good-quality bought puff pastry is fine if you don't want to make your own.

375 g puff pastry
1 egg, beaten
50 g mature Cheddar cheese, grated
150 g Gruyère or similar cheese, grated
600 g good-quality cooked ham, thinly sliced

For the béchamel sauce
25 g butter
25 g plain flour
150 ml milk
50 ml double cream
nutmeg
salt and freshly ground black pepper

FIRST, MAKE THE BÉCHAMEL by melting the butter until it foams. Mix in the flour and cook gently over a low heat for 4–5 minutes, not allowing it to colour.

WITH THE PAN STILL ON THE HEAT, slowly whisk in the milk and cream, then increase the heat and bring to the boil. Keep mixing well to avoid lumps and burning – the sauce should be quite thick.

SEASON LIGHTLY WITH SALT but quite generously with pepper and nutmeg. Pour into a container and cover with a buttered paper to avoid a crust forming. Set aside to cool completely.

ON A LIGHTLY FLOURED SURFACE, roll out half the pastry to a circle about 24 cm wide. Roll out another circle about 26 cm wide. Cover this one and keep cold.

PREHEAT THE OVEN to 200°C/Gas 6. Place the first pastry circle on a baking tray, brush the edges with beaten egg and put a spoonful of béchamel in the centre. Spread the sauce over the pastry to within 3–4 cm of the edges. Sprinkle over a little cheese, followed by some ham. Repeat these layers until all the ham, cheese and béchamel have been used up.

COVER THE FILLING with the chilled sheet of pastry and press down firmly around the edges. Trim neatly, brush with beaten egg and score the top with the point of a knife to decorate. Make a little hole in the top of the pie to let out the steam. Bake for 30 minutes, then turn the oven down to 180°C/Gas 4 and cook for another 15 minutes. Leave the pie to cool for at least 30 minutes before cutting into slices.

GORDON RAMSAY

Maple-and-mustard-glazed ham

SERVES 8—10

A succulent maple-glazed ham is perfect for a Boxing Day feast.

1 x 5 kg leg of gammon,
  smoked or unsmoked,
  bone in
1 cinnamon stick
1 tsp peppercorns
1 tsp coriander seeds
2 bay leaves
about 25 whole cloves

For the glaze
200 ml maple syrup
2 tbsp coarse-grain mustard
2 tbsp Worcestershire sauce
2 tbsp soy sauce

PUT THE GAMMON in a very large pan and cover with cold water. Add the cinnamon, peppercorn, coriander seeds and bay. Bring to the boil, then turn down and simmer for around 1 hour and 50 minutes, topping up with boiling water if necessary. Skim off any scum that rises to the top every now and then.

CAREFULLY DRAIN OFF the cooking liquid (I like to keep it for making soup), then let the ham cool a little while you heat the oven to 190°C/Gas 5. Lift the ham into a large roasting tin, then cut away the skin, leaving behind an even layer of fat. Score the fat all over in a criss-cross pattern, then stud cloves all over the ham. It can now be chilled for up to 2 days.

MIX THE GLAZE INGREDIENTS IN A JUG. Pour half over the prepared joint, then roast for 15 minutes. Pour the remaining glaze over the meat and return it to the oven for another 35 minutes, basting with the pan juices 3—4 times as it bakes. Turn the pan around a few times during cooking so that the fat colours evenly. Remove from the oven and allow to rest for 15 minutes before carving. The gammon can be roasted on the day, or up to 2 days ahead and served cold.

Trout with crispy bacon and almond sauce

SERVES 4

Here's an interesting variation on a well-used theme. In this version the almonds are made into a delicious sauce with leeks, garlic, cream and ginger wine.

4 small whole trout, gutted
8 thin rashers smoked
   streaky bacon
25 g butter
2 tbsp oil
25 g flaked almonds, toasted
parsley sprigs, to garnish

For the sauce
½ small leek, green part only
25 g butter
2 garlic cloves, crushed
25 g ground almonds
4 tbsp ginger wine
3 tbsp double cream
salt and freshly ground pepper

LIGHTLY SCORE THE FISH once or twice on each side. Wrap 2 rashers of bacon around each fish, securing in place with wooden cocktail sticks.

MELT THE BUTTER with the oil in a frying pan. Add the trout and fry gently for 5 minutes, until the bacon is crisp and golden. Turn and fry for a further 5 minutes, or until the fish is cooked through. Scatter the flaked almonds over the trout.

MEANWHILE, MAKE THE SAUCE. Trim and thinly slice the leek. Melt the butter in a saucepan. Add the leek and garlic and fry for 5 minutes, until the leeks are softened.

STIR IN THE GROUND ALMONDS and ginger wine and cook gently for 3 minutes, until the mixture forms a soft paste. Stir in the cream and season with salt and pepper to taste.

ARRANGE THE TROUT and almonds on warmed serving plates and add a generous spoonful of the sauce to each. Serve garnished with parsley.

Filo turrets of sole

SERVES 4

Here sole fillets are wrapped around a purée of prawns, ginger and dill, then enclosed in delicate leaves of filo pastry. The turrets are served on a pool of ginger butter sauce dotted with red 'jewels' of salmon caviar.

225 g raw prawns
  (thawed if frozen), chilled
2 spring onions, chopped
1.25 cm fresh root ginger,
  peeled and grated
2 tbsp chopped fresh dill
1 egg white, lightly beaten
3 tbsp whipping cream
4 double sole fillets
5 sheets filo pastry
75 g butter, melted
1 tbsp polenta or semolina flour
salt and freshly ground pepper

For the ginger sauce
1 shallot, finely chopped
4 thin slices of fresh root ginger
3 tbsp white wine vinegar
225 g unsalted butter,
  chilled and cubed
squeeze of lemon juice

To garnish
salmon caviar
shredded spring onion

FOR THE FILLING, process the prawns, onions, ginger and dill to a paste. With the machine running, pour in the egg white through the feeder tube and blend for 30 seconds. Add the cream in the same way and blend briefly until combined. Season.

SPREAD THIS PASTE EVENLY over each sole fillet and roll up from the thick end. Secure with a cocktail stick. Place in a shallow pan and pour in 150 ml water. Slowly bring to a bare simmer, cover tightly and turn off the heat. Leave for 10 minutes. Drain on kitchen paper. Cool.

CUT THE PASTRY into ten 20 cm squares and cover with a damp tea towel. Take two squares, brush with melted butter and place one on top of the other. Cut in half and place on top of each other to form a rectangle of four layers. Cut the rectangle into eight 2.5 cm squares — these will be the bases on which to sit the fish.

PREHEAT THE OVEN to 200°C/Gas 6. Take the fish rolls and trim one end of each so they will stand up. Butter one large square of filo. Place one layered square in the middle and sprinkle with polenta. Stand a fish roll on top, then bring the buttered filo up around it, twisting to secure. Frill out the top and place on a baking sheet. Repeat with the remaining fish and filo. Drizzle the parcels with butter and bake for 10–15 minutes.

MEANWHILE, PLACE THE SHALLOT in a small pan with the ginger, 3 tablespoons water and the vinegar. Boil until reduced to 2 tablespoons. Discard the ginger. Over a low heat, whisk in the butter, a piece at a time. Do not allow to boil. Add lemon juice and seasoning to taste.

SERVE TWO 'TURRETS' on each warmed plate on a pool of ginger butter sauce. Garnish with salmon caviar and spring onion shreds.

MARY BERRY

Baked cod with vine tomatoes and hollandaise sauce

SERVES 6

Cod is a perennially favourite fish, and it goes particularly well with the sweetness of vine tomatoes.

6 x 175 g tail fillets of cod, skinned
olive oil
30 small vine tomatoes
3 tablespoons Mary Berry's
   Hollandaise Sauce
salt and freshly ground pepper
6 basil sprigs, to garnish

PREHEAT THE OVEN to 220°C/Gas 7. Lightly grease a large baking tin.

SEASON THE COD FILLETS on both sides, then place in the greased baking tin. Drizzle olive oil over the fish.

CUT THE VINE TOMATOES into 6 pieces and place on top of the fillets. Bake in the oven for about 15 minutes, or until the fish has turned white.

GENTLY HEAT the hollandaise sauce in a small saucepan and serve with the cod, garnished with fresh basil leaves.

Tuna baked with artichokes and capers

SERVES 4

Here's a dish that can be eaten all year round as many of the ingredients are good store-cupboard standbys. Fish and capers are a classic combination, and here mildly flavoured tuna is given a further lift from the slightly tart artichokes.

2 tbsp olive oil
4 tuna steaks (about 125 g each)
3 garlic cloves, crushed
grated zest of 1 lemon
2 tbsp salted capers, drained
    and rinsed
4 tbsp finely chopped flatleaf
    parsley
1 x 280 g jar artichokes in oil,
    drained
200 ml white wine
100 ml hot fish stock
salt and freshly ground pepper

PREHEAT THE OVEN to 180°C/Gas 4.

HEAT THE OIL in a large frying pan over a high heat and fry the tuna steaks for about a minute on each side, until golden. Transfer to a baking dish.

ADD THE GARLIC, lemon zest, capers, parsley and artichokes to the dish. Pour over the wine and stock and season well. Cover with foil and cook in the oven for about 15 minutes. Serve piping hot.

Salmon en papillote with lime butter sauce

SERVES 4

In this delicious recipe, salmon steaks scented with lime and ginger are gently cooked in paper parcels, then served with a rich butter sauce flavoured with lime and dry sherry. The sauce can be made in advance and gently reheated in a bain-marie as the fish is cooking, making this recipe a perfect dinner party dish.

75 g unsalted butter
2 limes
15 g fresh root ginger
4 salmon steaks
   (about 175 g each)
4 spring onions, trimmed
pinch of sugar
3 tbsp dry sherry
   (preferably Manzanilla)
3 tbsp double cream
salt and freshly ground pepper

PREHEAT THE OVEN to 200°C/Gas 6. Cut 4 baking parchment or greaseproof paper rectangles measuring 30 x 20 cm. Using 25 g of the butter, grease the paper.

GRATE THE RIND from 1 lime and squeeze the juice. Peel the ginger, then cut into very fine slices.

PLACE A SALMON STEAK on one half of each paper rectangle. Season with salt and pepper. Scatter the lime rind and ginger on top, then sprinkle with the lime juice. Fold the other half of the paper over the top, brushing the edges together. Make small overlapping folds along the edges to seal. Place on a baking sheet and set aside.

TO MAKE THE SAUCE, chop the spring onions. Heat 15 g of the butter in a small pan, add the spring onions and cook until softened. Squeeze the juice from the remaining lime. Add to the onions with the sugar and sherry. Increase the heat and boil steadily until the liquid is reduced by half.

PLACE THE FISH PAPILLOTES in the oven and cook for 12–15 minutes; the parcels will puff up.

ADD THE CREAM to the sauce and allow to bubble for a few seconds. Gradually whisk in the remaining butter a piece at a time, taking the pan off the heat occasionally to prevent the sauce from splitting. The sauce should be smooth and slightly thickened. Season with salt and pepper.

SERVE THE PAPILLOTES at the table, allowing each person to enjoy the fragrance as they open their own parcel. Serve the sauce separately.

Salmon steaks with basil and balsamic vinegar

SERVES 4

This pretty dish is very quick and easy to prepare. The salmon is grilled with balsamic vinegar, which gives it a sweet-sour 'glaze'. The contrast of the hot salmon with the cool, firm tomatoes is sublime, especially when mingled with the basil oil.

4 salmon steaks
    (about 175 g each)
2 tbsp balsamic vinegar
2 tsp soy sauce
6 tbsp extra virgin olive oil
40 g fresh basil, stalks removed
8 ripe plum tomatoes
    (or other flavourful tomatoes)
2 tbsp chopped fresh chives
salt and freshly ground pepper

PLACE THE SALMON STEAKS in a shallow, non-metallic dish. Mix the balsamic vinegar and soy sauce together and pour over the salmon, turning to coat. Cover and leave to marinate in the fridge for 30 minutes.

MEANWHILE, place the olive oil and basil in a food processor or blender and work until smooth. Pour into a bowl, cover and leave to infuse. (Do not make this too far in advance.)

IMMERSE THE TOMATOES in a bowl of boiling water for 10 seconds. Remove with a slotted spoon and plunge into cold water. Slip off the skins, then halve the tomatoes and remove the seeds. Cut the flesh into fine dice and place in a bowl. Stir in the chives and season well with salt and pepper. Cover and set aside.

PREHEAT THE GRILL. Lift the salmon out of the marinade and place on a foil-lined grill pan. Grill the salmon steaks for 4 minutes on each side, brushing liberally with the marinade once on each side. If necessary, whisk the basil oil briefly at this stage to recombine.

SPOON A QUARTER of the tomato mixture onto each of four warmed serving plates and place a salmon steak on top. Drizzle some basil oil over each steak and spoon on any cooking juices. Serve immediately.

Haddock wrapped in Parma ham and spinach leaves

SERVES 2

While this beautiful dish makes a great centrepiece to a romantic meal for two, the quantities can easily be multiplied to make it for more people.

about 8 large spinach leaves
olive oil, for brushing
6–7 thin slices of Parma ham
350 g skinned haddock fillet
large pinch of freshly
   grated nutmeg
salt and freshly ground pepper

PREPARE A STEAMER and bring the water in it to a rolling boil. Add the spinach and steam for 1–2 minutes, until just wilted.

CUT A PIECE OF GREASEPROOF PAPER 1¼ times the length of the fish. Lay it horizontally on the work surface and brush it lightly with oil. Place the spinach leaves in a single layer on the paper, arranging them vertically and slightly overlapping, to make a rectangle the length of the paper. Cover the spinach with a layer of slightly overlapping Parma ham slices.

SEASON THE HADDOCK FILLET with nutmeg and salt and pepper, then sit it in the centre of the ham. Fold the narrow sides of the paper over the fish, then peel the paper off, leaving the ham and spinach covering the narrow ends of the fillet. Now fold the long side of paper closest to you over the fish, then peel it off, again leaving the ham and spinach on the fillet. Repeat with the final side of paper.

BRING THE WATER IN YOUR STEAMER to the boil again. Transfer the haddock to a heatproof plate that will fit in your steamer. Place the plate in the steamer, cover with a lid and steam over a medium heat for 8–9 minutes, until the flesh easily breaks into flakes. Cut the fish into thin slices and serve.

Monkfish stew with garlic

SERVES 6

Known as 'bourride' in French, this monkfish stew is a joy to cook and eat. Mopping up the broth with big chunks of bread at the end tastes almost too good to be true.

1.5 kg monkfish
4 tbsp olive oil
2 onions, thinly sliced
2 fennel bulbs, thinly sliced
2 carrots, thinly sliced
1 leek, white parts only, sliced
2 bay leaves
250 ml dry white wine
150 ml water
salt and freshly ground pepper

For the aïoli
10 garlic cloves
2 egg yolks
juice of 1 lemon
250 ml olive oil
1 tsp Dijon mustard

FIRST MAKE THE AÏOLI. Peel the garlic and remove the central 'germ' from the cloves. Place in a mortar or blender and pound or process, gradually adding all the other ingredients until you have a smooth paste. Set aside.

CLEAN THE MONKFISH, remove the outer membrane and cut into 6 equal pieces. Leave the pieces on the bone.

HEAT A LITTLE OLIVE OIL in a large pan and sweat the vegetables until tender. Add the bay leaves and a little seasoning. Pour over the wine and 150 ml water and simmer for about 10 minutes.

SEASON THE MONKFISH and fry in a non-stick pan over a high heat for only 3–4 minutes in total. Remove the fish from the pan and add to the vegetables. Cover with a loose-fitting lid and simmer for 8–10 minutes. When the fish is cooked, remove it with a slotted spoon and set aside.

WHISK THE AÏOLI into the vegetable broth. The vegetables should break up and the broth should take on a thick soup consistency. Do not re-boil once the aïoli has been incorporated or the mixture might separate.

SERVE IMMEDIATELY in deep bowls.

Grilled lobster

SERVES 4

This is a fabulous dish that I used to make when working in Barbados. Lobster's not my favourite shellfish as it can be chewy and quite tough, but this is a great way of cooking it: sear quickly on the grill pan, herb butter on top…bang — done! You could also cook it in the oven, at 220°C/ Gas 7 for 6–8 minutes, until soft.

2 live lobsters (about
   600–800 g each)
100 g softened butter
2 garlic cloves, finely chopped
½ tbsp chopped fresh
   flatleaf parsley
½ tbsp chopped fresh tarragon
olive oil, for drizzling
salt and freshly ground pepper

PLACE THE LOBSTERS in the freezer for a couple of hours while you tackle the first step. This will send them to sleep before you come to prepare them.

IN A BOWL MIX TOGETHER the butter, garlic and herbs. Season well and leave to set in the fridge. Once cold, dice into 5 mm cubes.

TAKE THE LOBSTERS out of the freezer. Position the point of a very sharp knife on the natural cross mark on the top of the head. Pressing hard, bring down the knife to make a horizontal cut. Then make a vertical cut between the lobster's eyes. This kills the lobster instantly. Cut down through the back of the head and tail. Remove the dark vein running along the back of the tail. Discard the dirt sac from the head, as well as any green coral, so that you are left with just the tail and claw meat. Drizzle a little olive oil on each lobster half and season.

HEAT A GRIDDLE PAN until hot and place the lobster halves on it, cut side down. Cook for 4–5 minutes, then turn over and place a few cubes of the herb butter on top. Finish grilling on the shell side for another 4–5 minutes. When cooked through, the lobster should be a bright red colour and the butter melted. Serve immediately.

Seared scallops with roasted plum tomatoes

SERVES 4

Here's a vibrant dish with all the colours, flavours and simplicity associated with Mediterranean food. A simple leafy salad, some good bread and a glass of chilled wine are all that's needed as accompaniment.

16 large fresh scallops, shelled
3 tbsp extra virgin olive oil
2 garlic cloves
2 tbsp chopped fresh thyme
    or parsley
coarse sea salt and freshly
    ground pepper

For the roasted tomatoes
6 large plum tomatoes
    (or other flavourful tomatoes)
3 rosemary sprigs
3 tbsp extra virgin olive oil
juice of 1 small lemon

PREHEAT THE OVEN to 180°C/Gas 4.

RINSE THE SCALLOPS and pat dry with kitchen paper. Place in a bowl and spoon over the olive oil. Crush the garlic cloves to a paste on a chopping board with a little coarse sea salt. Add to the scallops with the chopped thyme or parsley. Season with pepper and mix well. Cover and refrigerate while preparing the tomatoes.

CUT THE TOMATOES in half lengthways. Place them in one layer, cut side up, in a shallow baking tin. Add the rosemary and season liberally with sea salt. Drizzle over the olive oil. Roast in the preheated oven for about 45 minutes, until tender but still holding their shape.

ABOUT 10 MINUTES before the tomatoes are ready, preheat a large dry (not oiled) cast-iron griddle pan over a high heat for about 5 minutes. Lower the heat to medium.

TO COOK THE SCALLOPS, add them to the hot griddle pan in one layer. Allow to sizzle undisturbed for 1½ minutes, then turn each scallop and cook the other side for 1½ minutes.

TO SERVE, lift the tomatoes from the baking tin and arrange on four warmed serving plates with the scallops and rosemary sprigs.

POUR THE OIL from the tomatoes into the griddle pan and add the lemon juice. Stir well to scrape up all the flavoursome sediment in the bottom of the pan as it sizzles. Trickle the juices over the scallops and roasted plum tomatoes and serve at once.

Fish pie with saffron mash

SERVES 4—6

Here's another familiar dish with a difference: chunks of cod, prawns and mussels are cooked in a creamy sauce under a layer of golden-coloured, saffron-scented mashed potato. The pie is flavoured with fresh dill and tomato.

450 g cod fillet
450 ml milk
½ onion, sliced
1 bay leaf
225 g tomatoes
175 g cooked shelled prawns
175 g cooked shelled mussels
1 tbsp chopped fresh dill
50 g butter
25 g plain flour

For the saffron mash
1 kg floury potatoes
1 tsp saffron threads
1 garlic clove
75 g butter, melted
150 ml single cream
150 ml milk
salt and freshly ground pepper

PREHEAT THE OVEN to 180°C/Gas 4.

FIRST MAKE THE SAFFRON MASH. Peel the potatoes and cut into even-sized chunks. Put them in a pan with enough water to cover, add the saffron and garlic and bring to the boil. Cover and simmer until cooked.

MEANWHILE, lay the cod in an ovenproof dish, pour in the milk and add the onion and bay leaf. Cover and cook in the oven for 20 minutes, until the fish is firm. Strain off the milk and reserve.

WHILE THE POTATOES AND FISH are cooking, place the tomatoes in boiling water for 30 seconds, then refresh in cold water and peel away the skin. Cut into quarters, discard the seeds and roughly chop the flesh.

DRAIN THE POTATOES, retaining the saffron and garlic. Add the butter and mash until smooth. Add the cream and milk and beat until light and fluffy. Season.

TURN UP THE OVEN to 230°C/Gas 8. Flake the cod into a buttered ovenproof dish. Add the prawns, mussels and tomatoes. Scatter over the dill.

MELT 25 G BUTTER IN A PAN, add the flour and cook for 30 seconds. Stir in the reserved milk from the cod, and cook, stirring until thickened. Season with salt and pepper and pour over the fish.

SPOON THE SAFFRON MASH over the fish mixture, covering it completely. Dot with the remaining butter and bake in the oven for 10–15 minutes, until nicely browned on top.

Tarte au Roquefort

SERVES 6

The garlic and walnut topping on this wonderfully creamy tart is a must for all blue cheese lovers. A chicory, pear and watercress salad is the ideal complement.

225 g cream cheese, at room
   temperature
150 ml crème fraîche or
   double cream
3 eggs, beaten
175 g Roquefort cheese
freshly ground pepper
freshly grated nutmeg
3 tbsp chopped fresh chives

For the pastry
250 g plain flour
1 tsp salt
125 g butter, softened
1 egg yolk (size 1)

For the topping
2 tbsp olive oil
3 garlic cloves, sliced
125 g walnut halves
1 tbsp walnut oil
3 tbsp chopped fresh parsley

FIRST MAKE THE PASTRY. Sift the flour and salt onto a sheet of greaseproof paper. Put the butter and egg yolk in a food processor and blend until smooth. Shute in the flour and work until just combined. Turn onto a lightly floured work surface and knead gently until smooth. Form into a ball, flatten and wrap in clingfilm. Refrigerate for at least 30 minutes. Allow to come back to room temperature before rolling out.

BEAT THE CREAM CHEESE in a bowl until softened, then beat in the cream and eggs. Crumble in the Roquefort and mix gently. Season liberally with pepper and a little nutmeg. As the cheese is salty, you probably won't need to add more. Stir in the chives and set aside.

PREHEAT THE OVEN to 200°C/Gas 6.

ROLL OUT THE PASTRY on a lightly floured surface and use to line a 25 cm loose-bottomed flan tin. Chill for 20 minutes, then lightly prick the base with a fork. Line the base with greaseproof paper and baking beans or uncooked rice and bake blind for 10 minutes. Remove the paper and beans and bake for a further 5 minutes. Let cool slightly. Lower the oven setting to 190°C/Gas 5.

POUR THE FILLING into the pastry case and bake for 30—35 minutes, or until puffed and lightly browned.

MEANWHILE, make the topping. Heat the olive oil in a frying pan and add the garlic and walnuts. Stir-fry until the garlic is golden and the walnuts are browned. Stir in the walnut oil and parsley. Serve the tart warm or cold, sprinkled with the warm garlic and walnut topping.

Aubergine parmigiana

SERVES 4

This classic Italian dish is ideal for making in advance because it benefits from being left to rest overnight so that the flavours develop. Key to its success are a rich tomato sauce and thick aubergine slices. It makes a great starter, or a veggie main course with a green salad, but I also love to serve it as an accompaniment to lamb, chicken, sea bass or halibut.

200 ml olive oil
1 small onion, chopped
1 garlic clove, crushed
1 x 400 g tin plum tomatoes
2 large aubergines
2 x 125 g balls of buffalo
   mozzarella, sliced
bunch of fresh basil leaves
100 g Parmesan cheese,
   freshly grated
salt and freshly ground pepper

PUT 2 TABLESPOONS of the olive oil into a medium saucepan over a low heat. When hot, add the onion and garlic and cook for 3–4 minutes, until soft and translucent but not coloured.

ADD THE TOMATOES, break them up gently with a wooden spoon, and simmer for 25–30 minutes to create a thick sauce. Season to taste. Press the sauce through a sieve into a bowl and set to one side. Discard the pulp.

CUT THE AUBERGINES lengthways into 5 mm slices and sprinkle with a little salt. Leave for about 10 minutes to release their excess moisture. Pat dry with kitchen paper or a tea towel.

HEAT THE REMAINING OLIVE OIL in a large frying pan and shallow-fry the aubergine slices; they should be only lightly coloured.

PREHEAT THE OVEN to 190°C/Gas 5.

TO ASSEMBLE THE DISH, spoon a third of the tomato sauce into a shallow ovenproof dish (about 25 x 20 cm). Add a single layer of cooked aubergines, slightly overlapping the slices. Follow with a layer of sliced mozzarella, a handful of basil leaves and a sprinkling of Parmesan.

REPEAT THE PROCESS, finishing with a layer of aubergine. Sprinkle with the remaining Parmesan and cook in the oven for 25–30 minutes, until a lovely, bubbling crust has formed.

Sweet and sour vegetable noodles

SERVES 4

If you're put off by the luminous colour of take-away sweet and sour dishes, this easy homemade version will be a welcome alternative.

1 tbsp sunflower oil
1 large onion, thickly sliced
100 g cashew nuts
2 carrots, halved lengthways and
    sliced thickly on the diagonal
2 celery sticks, sliced
4 garlic cloves, chopped
30 g fresh root ginger, peeled
    and cut into matchsticks
pinch of chilli flakes
1 star anise
1 green pepper and 1 red pepper,
    thickly sliced
1 x 225 g tin water chestnuts
4 tbsp rice wine vinegar
4 tbsp mirin, rice wine or
    dry sherry
2 tbsp caster sugar
juice of 1 lemon
125 ml pineapple juice
2 tbsp cornflour
1 tbsp sesame oil
600 g cooked egg noodles
150 g mangetout, halved
8 spring onions, thinly sliced
    on the diagonal
salt and freshly ground pepper

PREHEAT THE OVEN to 180°C/Gas 4.

HEAT THE OIL in a large frying pan over a high heat and cook the onion for 2 minutes. Add the cashews, carrots, celery, garlic and ginger and cook for a further 2–3 minutes, until tinged with brown. Transfer to a casserole and scatter over the chilli flakes, star anise, peppers and water chestnuts.

IN A SMALL BOWL, combine the vinegar, mirin, sugar, lemon juice, pineapple juice and cornflour until smooth. Season well and pour the sauce into the casserole. Cook for 30 minutes.

ABOUT 10 MINUTES BEFORE the end of the cooking time, stir in the sesame oil, noodles and mangetout and continue to cook. Serve spooned into bowls and topped with the spring onions.

Wild mushrooms on field mushrooms with béarnaise sauce

SERVES 4

4 good-sized field mushrooms
about 2 tbsp olive oil
15 g butter
1 shallot, finely chopped
1 garlic clove, finely chopped
100 g shitake mushrooms, sliced
100 g oyster mushrooms, sliced
100 g chestnut mushrooms, sliced
4 tbsp Mary Berry's Béarnaise Sauce
1 tbsp chopped fresh parsley
salt and freshly ground pepper

PREHEAT THE OVEN to 180°C/Gas 4. Have ready a shallow ovenproof baking dish, just large enough to hold the mushrooms in a single layer.

TWIST THE STALKS from the field mushrooms. Wipe the caps with kitchen paper and slice the stalks.

HEAT THE OLIVE OIL in a frying pan. Fry the mushrooms gill-side down for about 5 minutes, turning them over halfway through the cooking time. Place them in the baking dish, season with salt and pepper, then cook in the oven for about 10 minutes.

ADD THE BUTTER TO THE PAN, stir in the shallot and cook over a moderate heat for about 3 minutes, or until the shallot begins to soften and colour. Add the garlic and continue cooking for 1 minute. Add the shiitake, oyster and chestnut mushrooms, and the sliced field mushroom stalks. Turn down the heat to low, cover and cook gently for about 5 minutes. Add the béarnaise sauce and continue to cook until the mushrooms are tender and the sauce has reduced to a nice coating consistency. Season with salt and pepper.

REMOVE THE PAN FROM THE HEAT. Spoon an equal amount of the mushrooms and sauce over each field mushroom, sprinkle with parsley and serve with toast.

Mushroom, chestnut and sourdough puddings

SERVES 4

A savoury take on the traditional sweet version of bread and butter pudding, these mushroom and chestnut puddings make a healthy and filling vegetarian main course.

2 tsp olive oil, plus extra
    for greasing
1 garlic clove, finely chopped
450 g mixed mushrooms,
    trimmed and sliced
3 fresh thyme sprigs, leaves
    roughly chopped
3 tbsp brandy
50 g vacuum-packed chestnuts,
    roughly chopped
150 g sourdough bread with
    crust, cut into olive-sized
    pieces
2 eggs
125 ml half-fat crème fraîche
150 ml semi-skimmed milk
1 tbsp wholegrain mustard
salt and freshly ground pepper

HEAT THE OLIVE OIL in a large frying pan over a high heat. Add the garlic, mushrooms and thyme and sauté for 2 minutes. Pour in the brandy and cook, stirring, until the mushrooms are tender and all the liquid has evaporated. Season with salt and pepper. Stir in the chestnuts and bread, then divide the mixture between 4 large ramekins.

BREAK THE EGGS into a jug and gently whisk in the crème fraîche, milk and mustard until well combined. Season with salt and pepper, then divide this custard mixture between the ramekins. Cover each dish with a piece of foil.

PREPARE A STEAMER and bring the water in it to a gentle simmer. Add the puddings, cover with a lid and steam for 15 minutes, or until just set. Serve immediately.

Carrot and coriander roulade

SERVES 4—6

An interesting and tasty dish, this carrot roulade is rolled around a filling of cream cheese flavoured with garlic, herbs and chopped coriander leaves. Serve it in slices with a mixed leaf and herb salad, and toasted granary or walnut bread.

50 g butter or vegetable margarine
450 g carrots, grated
4 eggs (size 2), separated
1 tbsp chopped coriander leaves
coarse sea salt and freshly ground pepper

For the filling
175 g soft cheese flavoured with garlic and herbs
1 tbsp chopped coriander leaves
2–3 tbsp crème fraîche

To serve
assorted salad leaves
herb sprigs, such as dill and chervil or parsley

PREHEAT THE OVEN to 200°C/Gas 6. Line a 30 x 20 cm Swiss roll tin with non-stick baking parchment.

MELT THE BUTTER or margarine in a pan. Add the carrots and cook gently, stirring frequently, for 5 minutes, or until slightly coloured. Transfer to a bowl, allow to cool slightly, then add the egg yolks and coriander and beat well. Season with salt and pepper.

WHISK THE EGG WHITES into firm peaks, then stir 2 tablespoons of them into the carrot mixture to lighten it. Carefully fold in the rest of the egg whites.

SPREAD THE MIXTURE evenly in the prepared tin and bake in the oven for 10—15 minutes, until risen and firm to the touch. Turn the 'sponge' out onto a sheet of non-stick baking parchment, cover with a clean, damp cloth and allow to cool.

MEANWHILE, prepare the filling. Put the soft cheese in a bowl. Using a fork, mix in the chopped coriander and enough crème fraîche to yield a smooth spreading consistency. Taste and adjust the seasoning if necessary.

REMOVE THE CLOTH from the baked 'sponge' and peel off the top layer of parchment. Spread evenly with the filling, leaving a 1 cm border all round. Carefully roll up from a short side, using the paper underneath to help.

TO SERVE, cut the roulade into slices and arrange on individual plates with the salad leaves and herbs.

Gnocchi and wild mushroom gratin

SERVES 4—6

This particular type of gnocchi is made with choux pastry and is called *à la Parisienne*.

360 g mixed wild mushrooms
olive oil
2 garlic cloves, crushed
60 g Cheddar cheese, grated
40 g Parmesan cheese, grated

For the choux pastry
100 g butter
pinch salt
pinch ground white pepper
1 tsp dried cep powder
    (optional)
125 g plain flour, sifted
3 free-range eggs

For the béchamel sauce
30 g butter
30 g plain flour
350 ml milk
1 thyme sprig
1 bay leaf
nutmeg
salt and freshly ground pepper

FIRST MAKE THE CHOUX PASTRY. Put 250 ml water in a saucepan, add the butter, seasoning and cep powder (if using) and bring to the boil. Take the pan off the heat and stir in the flour with a wooden spatula. When well mixed and smooth, return the pan to the heat. Cook the mixture over a medium flame, stirring vigorously, for 2—3 minutes; the bottom of the mixture should be starting to catch.

TAKE THE PAN OFF THE HEAT and beat in the eggs one at a time. This takes a long time.

PUT THE CHOUX PASTE in a piping bag with an 8 mm hole. Gently squeeze the bag over a pan of salted boiling water, using a small, sharp knife to cut the paste into roughly 1 cm lengths as it comes out.

SIMMER THE GNOCCHI for about 5 minutes, then lift out with a slotted spoon. Put straight into iced water to halt the cooking, then drain in a colander.

MELT THE BUTTER for the béchamel, add the flour and cook until foaming, but do not allow to colour. Slowly whisk in the milk over a high heat and add the herbs, nutmeg and seasoning. Bring to the boil, then simmer for 10 minutes. Take off the heat, pour through a fine sieve, cover and set aside.

PREHEAT THE OVEN to 200°C/Gas 6. Put the gnocchi and mushrooms in a large ovenproof dish. Pour over the béchamel and sprinkle with the cheese. Bake for 20 minutes, until golden brown.

Vegetarian lasagne

SERVES 6

The Mediterranean vegetable filling in this lasagne has a custard-like topping made from goats' cheese, eggs and cream.
Use the mild, soft young goats' cheese – Chèvre Frais – which is usually sold in tubs. Alternatively, you can use cream cheese or curd cheese instead.

4 red, orange or yellow peppers
2 medium aubergines
5 tbsp extra virgin olive oil
2 onions, chopped
4 garlic cloves, thinly sliced
5 tbsp red wine or water
3 tbsp chopped fresh oregano
6 tbsp sun-dried tomato purée
12 sheets dried lasagne
salt and freshly ground pepper

For the topping
350 g fresh soft goats' cheese
2 eggs
150 ml single cream
3 tbsp dry white breadcrumbs
2 tbsp freshly grated Parmesan
   cheese

PREHEAT THE GRILL to hot. Grill the whole peppers, turning now and then, until the skins are blackened all over – about 20 minutes. Allow to cool slightly, then remove the skin, holding the peppers over a bowl to catch the juices. Chop the flesh, discarding the seeds, and set aside with the juices.

WHILE THE PEPPERS ARE GRILLING, cut the aubergines into 1 cm dice. Place in a colander, rinse with cold water, then sprinkle liberally with salt. Leave for 20 minutes, to extract the bitter juices. Rinse again, then blanch in boiling water for 1 minute; drain well.

HEAT THE OIL in a large saucepan. Add the onions and cook, stirring, for about 8 minutes, until golden. Add the garlic and cook for a further 2 minutes. Add the wine and bubble for 1 minute, then stir in the aubergine, oregano and tomato purée. Cover and cook over a medium heat for 15–20 minutes, stirring frequently. Take off the heat and stir in the grilled peppers and seasoning.

PREHEAT THE OVEN to 190°C/Gas 5.

COOK THE LASAGNE in a large pan of boiling salted water until al dente. Drain, then drop into a bowl of cold water with 2 tablespoons oil to prevent the sheets from sticking together. Drain again and lay on a clean tea towel.

OIL A LARGE BAKING DISH. Spread one-third of the filling in the base, then cover with a layer of pasta, trimming to fit. Repeat this twice more.

TO MAKE THE TOPPING, place the goats' cheese in a bowl, add the eggs and beat well. Stir in the cream and some seasoning. Spread evenly over the lasagne. Sprinkle with the breadcrumbs and Parmesan, then bake for 35–40 minutes, until hot and lightly browned.

Root vegetable and lentil casserole

SERVES 6

The spicy combination of mixed root vegetables and assorted lentils makes an ideal winter supper dish. Serve it with plenty of warm crusty bread and a side salad or seasonal green vegetable, such as broccoli or spinach.

1 tsp cumin seeds
1 tbsp coriander seeds
1 tsp mustard seeds
25 g fresh root ginger
3 onions
450 g carrots
350 g leeks
350 g mooli (white radish)
450 g button mushrooms
3 tbsp olive oil
2 garlic cloves, crushed
¼ tsp ground turmeric
175 g split red lentils
50 g brown or green lentils
2 tbsp chopped coriander leaves
   (optional)
salt and freshly ground pepper
parsley sprigs, to garnish

PREHEAT THE OVEN to 180°C/Gas 4.

USING A PESTLE AND MORTAR (or a strong bowl and the end of a rolling pin) crush the cumin, coriander and mustard seeds. Peel and grate or finely chop the ginger.

SLICE THE ONIONS AND CARROTS. Clean the leeks thoroughly, then cut into slices. Peel and roughly chop the mooli. Halve the mushrooms if large.

HEAT THE OIL in a large flameproof casserole. Add the onions, carrots, leeks and mooli, and fry for 2–3 minutes, stirring constantly. Add the mushrooms, garlic, ginger, turmeric and crushed spices, and fry for a further 2–3 minutes, stirring.

RINSE THE LENTILS in a colander under cold running water, then drain. Stir the lentils into the casserole with 750 ml boiling water. Season with salt and pepper and return to the boil. Cover and cook in the oven for about 45 minutes, or until the vegetables and lentils are tender. Stir in the coriander (if using), and adjust the seasoning before serving, garnished with parsley.

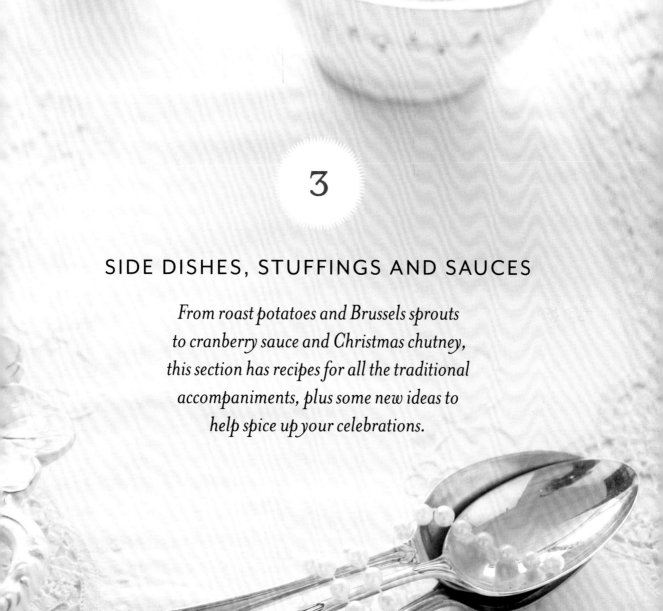

3

SIDE DISHES, STUFFINGS AND SAUCES

*From roast potatoes and Brussels sprouts
to cranberry sauce and Christmas chutney,
this section has recipes for all the traditional
accompaniments, plus some new ideas to
help spice up your celebrations.*

JAMIE OLIVER

Christmas vegetable mega mix

SERVES 6–8

This recipe uses the same principle as you'd use for roast potatoes — it's really a guide to get you thinking along the right lines and looking for fantastic flavour combos.

olive oil
sea salt and black pepper

500 g carrots
juice from 1 clementine, squeezed
   halves reserved
2 sprigs fresh rosemary, leaves
   picked

400 g parsnips
lug of white wine vinegar
2 sprigs fresh sage, leaves picked
1 small tsp honey

350 g baby turnips
couple of lugs of red wine vinegar
5 fresh bay leaves

2 fennel bulbs, quartered
2–3 sprigs fresh thyme, leaves
   picked
juice of ½ a lemon

350 g beets
2 lugs of balsamic vinegar
2–3 sprigs fresh oregano

IF ANY CARROTS, parsnips or turnips are big, halve them. Cut any larger beets into chunks. You can parboil all the veg together, except the beets — they'll turn everything red and also take longer to cook, around 20–25 minutes. Put the rest of the vegetables into a large pot, cover with cold water and season well. Bring to the boil and cook for about 6–7 minutes, until you've got part-cooked, softened bendy vegetables. Drain in a colander and leave to steam dry.

GET A SMALL TRAY and use it to mix up each set of vegetables with their own gorgeous flavours, a few good lugs of oil and a good pinch of salt and pepper. Toss the carrots, clementines and rosemary first and move them to a larger roasting tray so they're all together. Mix your fennel with its flavours and do the same with the others. When you get to the parsnips, keep the honey back for later. Make sure each group of veg is separate in the roasting tray. Cover the tray with tin foil and keep in the fridge until your turkey is cooked and resting.

TO COOK, PREHEAT YOUR oven to 190°C/Gas 5. Roast the vegetables in the hot oven for 50–60 minutes, or until golden, crispy and beautiful. For the last 5 minutes, drizzle the honey over the parsnips and jiggle the tray so they are nicely coated.

PILE ALL THE VEG up on a platter so they sprawl and hang all over the place. That platter is like winter in a nutshell, and every single mouthful will taste different and exciting — you'll definitely want to keep it close to you at the table.

Potatoes, fennel and celery with a mint and orange-water dressing

SERVES 4 (OR 2 AS A MAIN COURSE)

Try this fragrant dish with a spicy accompaniment to help counteract the heat and cleanse the palate. Alternatively, serve it as a vegetarian main course with freshly steamed couscous.

350 g new potatoes, scrubbed and sliced 2 cm thick
3 celery sticks, cut into 5 cm pieces
2 fennel bulbs, cut into thin wedges
2 garlic cloves, sliced
grated rind of 1 lemon
2 tsp orange blossom water
2 tsp extra virgin olive oil
handful of fresh mint leaves
salt and freshly ground pepper

PLACE THE POTATOES, celery, fennel and garlic in a shallow, heatproof dish that will fit in your steamer. Toss in the lemon rind and season with salt and pepper.

BRING THE WATER in your steamer to a rolling boil. Place the dish of vegetables inside the steamer, cover with a lid and steam for 10 minutes.

BEING CAREFUL NOT TO BURN YOURSELF, stir in the orange blossom water and olive oil, re-cover, and cook for a further 3—4 minutes, until the vegetables are tender. Toss in the mint leaves and serve.

Spiced potatoes and cauliflower

SERVES 4

Everyone's favourite vegetable curry, this combination of cauliflower and potato, known as aloo gobi, makes a delicious side dish. Alternatively, it can be served as a vegetarian main course, but you might wish to double the quantities.

450 g waxy potatoes
450 g cauliflower florets
1 onion
5 cm piece fresh root
    ginger, peeled
1 hot green chilli
4 tbsp ghee or vegetable oil
1 tsp black mustard seeds
1 tsp cumin seeds
1 tsp ground cumin
½ tsp ground turmeric
salt and freshly ground pepper

PEEL THE POTATOES and cut into large chunks. Place in a saucepan with enough salted water to cover, bring to the boil and boil for 5 minutes. Drain.

MEANWHILE, cut the cauliflower into smaller florets if necessary. Finely chop the onion and ginger. Finely slice the chilli, discarding the seeds if a milder flavour is preferred.

HEAT THE GHEE or oil in a large frying pan. Add the onion and ginger and cook over a medium heat until the onion is golden brown but not burnt. Add the chilli and spices and cook for 2 minutes, stirring all the time.

ADD THE POTATOES AND CAULIFLOWER, stirring to coat them in the spice mixture. Season with salt and pepper and stir in 3 tablespoons water. Cover with a lid and cook gently over a medium heat for about 10 minutes, or until the potatoes and cauliflower are tender. Check the pan occasionally during cooking, adding a little extra water if necessary to prevent sticking. Don't overcook the vegetables; they should retain their shape.

Shredded Brussels sprouts with bacon

SERVES 4

These buttery shredded sprouts are stir-fried with crispy cubes of bacon. They make an interesting change from traditional boiled or steamed Brussels sprouts and look so attractive. Use lightly smoked bacon, buying it in a piece if possible.

700 g Brussels sprouts
1 x 175 g piece smoked bacon
50 g butter
4 tbsp double cream
2 tsp caraway seeds
freshly grated nutmeg
salt and freshly ground pepper

TRIM THE SPROUTS and shred them very finely. Remove the rind from the bacon, then cut into small cubes.

HEAT A WOK or frying pan and add the bacon. Cook over a high heat, stirring all the time, until the fat runs and the bacon is browning and crisp. Stir in the butter.

ADD THE SPROUTS and stir-fry over a high heat for 2–3 minutes, until they begin to wilt.

POUR IN THE CREAM, add the caraway seeds and stir-fry for 1 minute. Season with nutmeg, salt and pepper. Transfer to a warmed serving dish and serve immediately.

Quick braised lettuce and peas

SERVES 6

As Gordon proves, good cooking doesn't have to be complicated.

16 halved pearl onions
300 g frozen peas
2 tbsp olive oil
3 baby Gem lettuces, finely shredded
salt and freshly ground pepper

COOK THE PEARL ONIONS for 5 minutes and the peas for 2 minutes in separate pans of boiling water until the onions are soft and the peas are just cooked.

HEAT THE OLIVE OIL in a frying pan, brown the onions, then add the peas and shredded lettuce. Cook just to heat through the lettuce, then season and serve.

Root vegetable mash

SERVES 6

1.5 kg potatoes, diced
500 g carrots, diced
500 g celeriac, diced
100 g butter
150 g pancetta, diced
salt and freshly ground pepper
2 tbsp chopped flatleaf parsley, to garnish

PUT THE POTATOES, carrots and celeriac in a pan of salted water and bring to the boil. Boil for about 20 minutes, or until very tender. Drain the vegetables and mash well, adding more seasoning. Stir in the butter and keep warm.

FRY THE PANCETTA in a dry pan over a medium heat, stirring constantly.

GARNISH THE ROOT VEGETABLE MASH with the chopped parsley and fried pancetta. Serve piping hot.

Parsnips with five spice and honey

SERVES 6

While this recipe is a great accompaniment to Christmas poultry, it's also fantastic with any roast meat.

750 g parsnips
oil
butter
good pinch of five-spice powder
a little vegetable stock
1 tbsp honey

PEEL THE PARSNIPS and cut into halves or quarters, depending on their size (cut out the cores if woody).

PUT A LITTLE OIL and a knob of butter in a large frying pan and, when it starts to sizzle, add the parsnips, a good pinch of five-spice powder and a little vegetable stock. Cook, turning regularly, until the parsnips are cooked through and browned on the outside.

ADD THE HONEY AND TOSS TOGETHER to give a caramelised coating. Season well.

Parsnip purée

SERVES 6

A creamy parsnip purée is the perfect accompaniment to a glorious roast bird.

900 g parsnips
3 tbsp double cream

PEEL THE PARSNIPS and cut into 7.5 cm chunks; cut these lengthways into finger-width pieces. Put the parsnips into a saucepan and cover with water. Bring to the boil, lower the heat and simmer for about 15 minutes, until completely tender.

DRAIN THOROUGHLY and return to the pan. Add the cream and seasoning and mash well until completely smooth.

Chickpeas with spinach

SERVES 4–6

This accompaniment goes well with most meat curries, but is also good with any hearty stew.

225 g dried chickpeas, or
   2 x 425 g tins chickpeas
4 tomatoes
3 tbsp ghee or vegetable oil
2.5 cm piece fresh root ginger,
   peeled and finely chopped
3 garlic cloves, crushed
2 tsp ground coriander
1 tsp ground cumin
2 tsp paprika
handful of fresh coriander
   leaves, roughly torn
450 g spinach leaves,
   trimmed and chopped
salt and freshly ground pepper
coriander sprigs, to garnish

IF USING DRIED CHICKPEAS, pick over them, discarding any small stones or shrivelled peas. Rinse thoroughly in plenty of cold running water, then put into a bowl, cover generously with cold water and leave to soak overnight.

DRAIN THE DRIED CHICKPEAS, put them in a large saucepan with plenty of water and bring to the boil. Lower the heat and simmer gently for 2–3 hours, or until tender, adding salt to taste towards the end of the cooking time. Drain well.

IF USING TINNED CHICKPEAS, simply drain and rinse under cold running water.

IMMERSE THE TOMATOES in boiling water for 30 seconds, then plunge into ice-cold water and peel off the skin. Cut in half, discard the seeds and finely chop the flesh.

HEAT THE GHEE OR OIL in a large, heavy-based saucepan or casserole. Add the ginger, garlic and spices and cook for 2 minutes, stirring all the time. Add the chickpeas and stir to coat in the spice mixture.

ADD THE TOMATOES, torn coriander and spinach. Cook for 2 minutes, then cover with a lid and simmer gently for 10 minutes. Season with salt and pepper, and garnish with coriander before serving.

Sugarsnap peas in a minted lemon dressing

SERVES 4

Sugarsnap peas are available all year round and make an excellent accompaniment. Here they are served in a light crème fraîche dressing flavoured with fresh mint and lemon.

400–450 g sugarsnap peas
4 tbsp crème fraîche
1 tbsp finely shredded or
    chopped fresh mint
juice and finely pared or
    grated rind of ½ lemon
90 ml natural yoghurt
coarse sea salt and freshly
    ground pepper
mint sprigs, to garnish

TOP AND TAIL the sugarsnap peas, then steam or cook them in boiling water until just tender.

MEANWHILE, gently heat the crème fraîche in a small saucepan, then add the mint, lemon juice and rind, stirring gently. When the sauce is warmed through, add the yoghurt; do not overheat at this stage or the sauce might curdle. Season with salt and pepper to taste.

DRAIN THE SUGARSNAPS and transfer to a warmed serving dish. Pour over the minted lemon sauce. Garnish with the mint sprigs and serve at once.

Caramelised leeks

SERVES 4

Pork and leek is a combination that never fails, so try these leeks with any pork recipe in this book.

30 g butter
2 leeks, finely sliced
2 tbsp demerara sugar

HEAT THE BUTTER in a frying pan over a medium heat and cook the leeks, stirring often, until really soft and golden.

STIR IN THE SUGAR and, when melted, remove from the heat. Serve straight away with your favourite pork dish.

Broccoli with lemon, chilli and almonds

SERVES 4

A fragrant dish that also works well with asparagus or French beans.

450 g tenderstem broccoli
roughly grated rind of 1 lemon
1 tsp olive oil
small pinch of crushed
   dried chillies
2 tbsp flaked almonds
salt and freshly ground pepper

PREPARE A STEAMER and bring the water in it to a rolling boil. Sit the broccoli on the perforated rack, scatter with the lemon rind and season with salt and pepper. Cover and steam for 3–4 minutes, until just tender.

MEANWHILE, heat the oil in a small frying pan over a medium heat. Add the chillies and almonds and fry, stirring, until the almonds begin to take on a golden colour. Spoon over the steamed broccoli and serve.

Peperonata

SERVES 2

A brilliantly versatile dish, this can be made in advance and kept in the fridge, served cold or hot, on its own or as an accompaniment. The flavour intensifies overnight, so it will taste even better the next day or several days later (don't keep it for longer than about a week, though). I like to serve it with roast lamb or monkfish. It also makes a great topping for Bruschette (page 204).

HEAT THE OLIVE OIL in a pan and add the onion. Cook until soft and translucent, but without colouring, about 3–4 minutes.

ADD THE PEPPERS and continue to cook gently until softened, again avoiding any colouring. Season to taste and add the tomatoes. Continue to cook over a low heat until the peppers are soft, about 1–1¼ hours. If the peppers look dry at any point, add a touch of water.

REMOVE THE PAN FROM THE HEAT, stir in the parsley and basil (if using) and it's ready to serve.

50 ml olive oil
1 small onion, sliced
3 red peppers, deseeded and chopped into 2 cm pieces
3 yellow peppers, deseeded and chopped into 2 cm pieces
1 x 400 g tin plum tomatoes
2 tbsp chopped fresh flatleaf parsley (optional)
2 tbsp chopped fresh basil (optional)
salt and freshly ground pepper

Courgette and rice stuffing

SERVES 10

Looking for a different kind of stuffing for your Christmas bird? This one is moist and tasty — you won't be disappointed.

115 g butter
1 small onion, finely chopped
2 garlic cloves, finely chopped
2 small leeks, thinly sliced
1 large courgette, coarsely grated
50 g long-grain white rice
50 g macadamia nuts or skinned hazelnuts, toasted
1 small eating apple
50 g well-flavoured Cheddar cheese
50 g seedless raisins
finely grated rind and juice of 1 lemon
75 g fresh white breadcrumbs
8 tbsp chopped fresh mixed herbs, such as parsley, chives and thyme
1 egg, beaten
salt and freshly ground pepper

HEAT HALF THE BUTTER in a heavy-based pan, add the onion, garlic and leeks and cook, stirring, for 2–3 minutes, until beginning to soften. Cover tightly and cook gently for a further 10 minutes, or until the leeks are quite soft. Add the courgette and cook for 2 minutes.

MEANWHILE, cook the rice in a large pan of boiling salted water until just tender. Drain in a sieve and rinse with plenty of boiling water.

MIX TOGETHER the softened vegetables, rice and nuts. Peel the apple and grate the flesh into the mixture. Grate in the cheese too. Add the raisins, lemon rind and juice, the breadcrumbs and herbs. Season with plenty of salt and pepper. Add just enough beaten egg to bind the stuffing — don't make it too wet.

USE TO STUFF A BIRD, or cook in a covered dish.

Tip

Other delicious stuffings can be found on pages 40, 70, 75 and 77.

Bread sauce

SERVES 8

4 whole cloves
1 onion
1 small bay leaf
600 ml milk
125g fresh white breadcrumbs
15 g butter
3 tbsp single cream (optional)
salt and freshly ground
    white pepper

STICK THE CLOVES into the onion and place in a small, heavy-based pan with the bay leaf and milk. Bring slowly to the boil, remove from the heat, cover and leave to infuse for 10 minutes.

REMOVE THE ONION and bay leaf, then add the breadcrumbs and seasoning to the milk. Return to the heat and simmer gently for 10–15 minutes, stirring occasionally. Stir in the butter and cream, if using, before serving.

Cranberry sauce

SERVES 8–10

This classic accompaniment to roast turkey can be served warm or cold. It has a fresh and chunky texture – so much nicer than the ready-made variety.

350 g fresh or frozen cranberries
175g caster sugar
finely grated zest and juice
    of 1 orange
150 ml orange juice
150 ml red wine

PLACE THE CRANBERRIES, sugar, orange juices and wine in a pan and simmer, uncovered, for 30 minutes, stirring occasionally.

USING A SLOTTED SPOON, transfer half the cranberries to a bowl and set aside.

PUT THE REST OF THE SAUCE in a blender or food processor and whizz until smooth. Combine with the reserved cranberries and the orange zest. Serve warm or cold.

MARY
BERRY

Christmas chutney

MAKES ABOUT 2.5 KG

A perfect match for cheese and cold meats, and delicious in turkey sandwiches.

900 g tomatoes
1 large aubergine, 3 red peppers
   and 1 green pepper
   (total weight about 900 g)
700 g onions, fairly finely
   chopped
4 fat garlic cloves, crushed
350 g granulated sugar
300 ml white wine vinegar
   or distilled malt vinegar
1 tbsp salt
1 tbsp coriander seeds, crushed
1 tbsp paprika
2 tsp cayenne pepper

PRICK THE TOMATOES with a sharp knife, place in a bowl and cover with boiling water. Leave for 30 seconds, then drain and cover with cold water. The skin will now come away easily.

CHOP THE TOMATOES and aubergine. Seed and chop the peppers. Put in a large heavy-based pan with the onions and garlic and bring to the boil. Cover with a lid, lower the heat and gently simmer for about 1 hour, stirring occasionally, until tender.

TIP THE SUGAR, vinegar, salt, coriander seeds, paprika and cayenne into the pan and bring to the boil over a medium heat, stirring, until the sugar has dissolved. Continue to boil for 30 minutes or so, until the mixture achieves a chunky consistency and the surplus watery liquid has evaporated. Take care towards the end of the cooking time to continue stirring so that the chutney doesn't catch on the bottom of the pan.

LADLE THE CHUTNEY into sterilised or dishwasher-clean jars (Kilner jars are ideal) and top with paper jam covers. Seal the jars while still hot. Leave to mature for at least a month in a cool dark place.

4

LEFTOVERS

*Say goodbye to never-ending mounds
of turkey sandwiches and hello to a fantastic
array of ideas for using up the remnants of
your festive food. They're so good that
you'll want to make lots of 'leftovers'.*

JAMIE
OLIVER

Leftover turkey and leek pie

SERVES 6—8

This is dead simple, completely versatile and absolutely gorgeous.

2 rashers quality smoked streaky bacon, roughly chopped
½ bunch fresh thyme, leaves picked
olive oil
large knob of butter
2 kg leeks, white end chopped into chunks, green end finely sliced
sea salt and freshly ground black pepper
800 g cooked white turkey meat, torn into big chunks (brown too if you want)
2 heaped tbsp plain flour, plus extra for dusting
1.2 litres organic turkey, chicken or vegetable stock
2 tbsp crème fraîche
1 x 500 g packet puff pastry
12 jarred or vac-packed chestnuts, roasted and peeled
2 sprigs fresh sage, leaves picked
1 large free-range egg, beaten

PREHEAT YOUR OVEN to 190°C/Gas 5. Put your bacon in a large pan on a medium heat with the thyme leaves. Add a lug of oil and the butter and fry for a few minutes. Add the leeks and fry for about 3 minutes so they are well coated in the butter. Season, then pop the lid on, turn the heat down slightly and let them cook away gently for 30 minutes, stirring every 5 minutes so they don't catch.

WHEN THE LEEKS ARE READY, add the turkey and any leftover stuffing you have, and stir. Add the flour, mix well then pour in your stock and stir again. Add the crème fraîche then turn the heat up and bring everything back to the boil. Taste and season if needed, then turn the heat off. Pour the mixture through a sieve set over another large empty pan and let the wonderful gravy drip through.

GET A DEEP BAKING DISH, roughly 22 x 30cm. Dust a clean surface and roll your pastry out so it's double the size of your dish. Crumble the chestnuts over half of the pastry and tear over a few of the sage leaves. Fold the other half over and roll it out so it's big enough to cover your dish.

SPOON THE FILLING from the sieve into the dish and spread evenly. Lay the pastry on top, tuck the ends under, then gently score diagonally with a knife. Add a pinch of salt to the beaten egg paint over the pastry. Pop the pie in the oven for about 35—40 minutes, or until the pastry is puffed up and golden brown. When ready, reheat the lovely gravy and serve with your pie, along with some green veg and everyone's happy!

AINSLEY HARRIOTT

Crispy ham and turkey hash with soft poached egg

SERVES 4

Waste not want not! This tastes so good that it's hard to believe it's leftovers.

3 tbsp olive oil
1 medium onion, diced
8–10 cooked leftover potatoes, roughly diced
about 250 g cooked turkey
100 g ham or bacon lardons
about 5 tbsp gravy
3 tbsp white vinegar
4 eggs
1 handful parsley, chopped
salt and freshly ground pepper

ADD OLIVE OIL to a large frying pan and, over a medium heat, fry the onion and potatoes in the oil for 8–10 minutes, stirring and tossing every now and then.

CUT THE TURKEY into small pieces and dice up equal quantities of ham (or use bacon lardons). Add to the pan and continue to fry until cooked through. Now add the gravy and continue to sauté, occasionally scraping the sediment from the bottom of the pan, until you have a crisp, golden hash. Taste and season.

MEANWHILE, poach the eggs. Bring a large pan of water (about 6–8 cm deep) to the boil and add the vinegar. Lower the heat to a simmer. Break each egg into a cup and slide into the water one by one. Poach for about 4 minutes, then remove with a slotted spoon.

DIVIDE THE HASH between four plates and sprinkle with chopped parsley. Sit a poached egg on top and serve straight away.

Turkey meatballs with red pepper sauce

SERVES 4

For the meatballs, you must use fresh turkey mince. If you want to use leftover turkey, simply chop it and warm through in the cooked sauce for 5–10 minutes before serving.

400 g turkey mince
1 egg white
1 x 290 g jar red peppers in brine, drained
500 g tomato passata
2 tbsp oil
2 garlic cloves, crushed
1 tsp cayenne pepper
1 x 400 g tin cannellini beans, drained and rinsed
1 large thyme sprig, leaves chopped
salt and freshly ground black pepper

To serve
600 g spaghetti
green salad

SEASON THE MINCE and stir in the egg white to bind. Divide the mixture into 12 pieces and roll in your hands to form 12 meatballs.

BLEND THE RED PEPPERS and passata together in a blender or food processor until well combined. Season.

HEAT THE OIL in a large frying pan over a high heat and cook the meatballs for about 2 minutes, until just brown all over. Add the garlic for the second minute.

ADD THE BLENDED RED PEPPERS to the pan, along with the cayenne, beans and thyme. Cover and cook gently for about 30 minutes.

JUST BEFORE SERVING, cook the spaghetti according to the packet instructions. Drain and serve with the meatballs and sauce, with a green salad on the side.

Turkey with black olives, tomatoes and basil

SERVES 4

Turkey tastes delicious in this traditional Italian sauce of olives, tomatoes and basil. For a truly authentic meal, serve it with your favourite fresh pasta.

2 tbsp olive oil
2 onions, roughly chopped
1 carrot, chopped
2 garlic cloves, left whole
about 500 g leftover turkey
1 tbsp tomato purée
500 g tomato passata
100 g pitted black olives, sliced
sea salt and freshly
    ground pepper
15 g basil leaves, to serve

HEAT THE OIL in the frying pan and cook the onions, carrot and garlic over a medium heat for 5 minutes.

ADD THE TURKEY MEAT, then stir in the tomato purée, passata, olives and seasoning. Cover and cook gently for about 40 minutes. Serve with pasta and garnish with basil.

Harissa turkey stew

SERVES 4

This light yet satisfying dish is inspired by North African cuisine; it has a real kick thanks to the fiery and vibrant harissa paste. Plain couscous makes the perfect accompaniment to this flavoursome stew.

4 turkey breast steaks (or about 500 g leftover turkey)
2 tbsp oil
2 red onions, roughly chopped
2 carrots, roughly chopped
4 garlic cloves, left whole
1 small preserved lemon, roughly chopped
1 tbsp tomato purée
250 g tomato passata
1 cinnamon stick
4 tbsp chopped coriander leaves
sea salt and freshly ground pepper

To serve
couscous
harissa paste
natural yoghurt

SEASON THE TURKEY STEAKS. Heat half the oil in a large frying pan over a high heat and brown the meat on both sides. Transfer to a plate.

HEAT THE REMAINING OIL in the frying pan and cook the onions, carrots and garlic over a medium heat for 5 minutes.

ADD THE PRESERVED LEMON, then stir in the tomato purée, passata, cinnamon and seasoning. Return the turkey to the pan, then cover and cook gently for 20 minutes.

JUST BEFORE SERVING, prepare the couscous according to the packet instructions. Stir the coriander into the stew and serve hot over the couscous with some harissa paste and yoghurt in separate bowls to be passed around.

MARY BERRY

Spicy turkey fajïtas

SERVES 6

A very easy supper dish that can be prepared ahead. The leftover turkey does not need cooking — just half an hour in the marinade. Then it can be added to the spring onions and red pepper.

12 wheat tortillas or fajitas
about 700 g leftover turkey
 or chicken breast, cut into
 thin chunks
5 tbsp Mary Berry's
 All Seasons Sauce

For frying
olive oil
8 spring onions, finely sliced
 on the diagonal
1 large red pepper, thinly sliced
salt and freshly ground pepper

To serve
mango chutney
soured cream or crème fraîche
cos lettuce, thinly sliced

PREHEAT THE OVEN to 160°C/Gas 3.

MARINATE THE TURKEY in a bowl with the All Seasons Sauce. Leave for 30 minutes, or longer if time allows.

WRAP 12 TORTILLAS IN FOIL and put into the oven for about 5 minutes to warm.

HEAT A LITTLE OIL in a frying pan. Using a slotted spoon, lift the turkey from the marinade and fry in batches with the spring onions and red pepper until golden brown and cooked through. Return all the meat to the pan, and cook for a further few minutes. Pour over any remaining marinade from the bowl and cook for a further minute.

PUT THE MANGO CHUTNEY, sour cream and lettuce in three separate bowls. Place the warm tortillas in a basket, and spoon the meat into a serving dish. Allow people to help themselves, or prepare the rolls yourself. Spread a fajita with mango chutney and soured cream, then add some of the spicy turkey and top with lettuce. Roll up and slice in half on the diagonal.

Turkey pasta sauce with sweet potato and rosemary

SERVES 4

Sometimes a hearty pasta sauce is needed on a cold winter evening, and this recipe has the advantage of using up leftover turkey too. The sauce has all the texture of the sweet potato and the flavour of the rosemary for the pasta to soak up.

400 g leftover turkey meat
3 tbsp olive oil
2 garlic cloves
2 tbsp finely chopped rosemary
400 g sweet potatoes, peeled and chopped
2 leeks, chopped
200 ml hot chicken stock
100 ml crème fraîche
salt and freshly ground pepper

To serve
300 g pasta
4 tbsp finely chopped flatleaf parsley
freshly grated Parmesan cheese

SEASON THE TURKEY MEAT. Heat half the oil in a large frying pan over a medium heat. Fry the meat until lightly golden, then transfer to a plate.

CHOP TOGETHER THE GARLIC and rosemary with a bit of salt. Heat the remaining oil in the frying pan and soften the sweet potatoes, leeks and rosemary and garlic.

RETURN THE TURKEY to the pan, add the stock, then cover and cook gently for about 30 minutes.

JUST BEFORE SERVING, cook the pasta according to the packet instructions.

STIR THE CRÈME FRAÎCHE into the sauce and heat through. Serve hot, spooned over the pasta and garnished with the parsley and Parmesan.

GORDON
RAMSAY

Bubble and squeak cakes

SERVES 8

These scrumptious potato cakes are perfect for serving with your Boxing Day ham (page 80).

1 kg floury potatoes (I use King Edwards), quartered
40 g butter
500 g Brussels sprouts, trimmed
50 g plain flour, seasoned with salt and pepper
olive oil, for frying

BOIL THE POTATOES for 12–15 minutes, or until tender, then drain and return to the pan over a low heat for 1–2 minutes to dry out. Add the butter and mash well.

WHILE THE POTATOES ARE COOKING, boil the sprouts for 3–5 minutes, until just tender. Drain and cool quickly under cold running water. Shake dry, then shred as finely as you can.

MIX THE SPROUTS with the potatoes and season to taste. Leave until cool enough to handle, then shape into 8 round cakes. Tip the flour on to a plate and coat the cakes in it, tapping off the excess.

HEAT A 5 MM DEPTH OF OIL in a large frying pan and cook the cakes in two batches for 2 minutes on each side, turning carefully. Drain on kitchen paper and transfer to a baking sheet lined with greaseproof paper. Cool, cover and chill or freeze. The cakes will keep in the fridge for up to 3 days or freeze for up to a month.

HEAT THE OVEN to 190°C/Gas 5 (or if you've roasted the ham, leave the oven on while it rests) and reheat the cakes for 15 minutes, until hot through and crisp on the outside.

Turkey, potato and spinach frittata

SERVES 4

For this tempting frittata, choose waxy potatoes, such as Wilja, Belle de Fonteney and Maris Bard, that hold their shape when sautéd. Also, use a good heavy-based frying pan to cook the frittata, or it will stick.

about 4 tbsp olive oil
450 g waxy potatoes, peeled and cut into 2.5 cm chunks
2 onions, halved and sliced
1 garlic clove, crushed (optional)
225 g cooked turkey meat, cut into bite-sized pieces
handful of baby spinach leaves or 1 large courgette
freshly grated nutmeg
5 eggs (size 1), beaten
salt and freshly ground pepper

HEAT HALF THE OIL in a heavy-based, preferably non-stick, frying pan. Add the potatoes, onions and garlic, if using. Cook over a high heat until the vegetables are tinged with brown. Lower the heat and continue cooking, stirring occasionally, until the potatoes are cooked. If the mixture starts to stick, add a little more oil.

WHEN THE POTATOES ARE COOKED, add the meat and cook over a high heat for 5 minutes, or until the turkey is heated through.

MEANWHILE, trim the spinach or slice the courgette. Add to the pan and season with nutmeg, salt and pepper. If using courgette, cook for a further 2 minutes to soften.

ADD A LITTLE EXTRA OIL to coat the bottom of the pan if necessary. Heat for 1 minute, then add the beaten eggs. Continue cooking over a high heat for about 2 minutes to set the egg on the bottom, then lower the heat and cook until the egg is just set on top.

REMOVE THE PAN from the heat and carefully use a palette knife to loosen the frittata around the edge. Invert a plate over the pan, then turn the plate and pan over to release the frittata. Slide the frittata back into the pan and cook for another 1–2 minutes. Serve immediately accompanied by a tomato salad and crusty bread.

Christmas pudding cupcakes

MAKES 12

2 eggs
150 ml milk
60 g butter, melted
3–4 tbsp brandy
250 g leftover
    Christmas pudding
250 g plain flour
1 tbsp baking powder
1 tsp mixed spice
150 g caster sugar

For the butter icing
250 g sifted icing sugar
100 g butter, softened
few drops vanilla extract

PREHEAT THE OVEN to 180°C/Gas 4. Line a 12-hole cupcake tin with paper cases.

WHISK THE EGGS in a large bowl, then add the milk, butter, brandy and Christmas pudding.

SIFT THE FLOUR, baking powder and mixed spice into another bowl. Add the caster sugar and mix well. Make a well in the centre, then add the egg mixture and stir well. Spoon the batter into the paper cases and bake for 20–25 minutes. Set aside to cool.

MEANWHILE, CREAM THE SUGAR and butter together for the icing, then add just enough vanilla to make it spreadable.

ONCE THE CUPCAKES are cool, spread the icing over the top and serve.

Buttery Christmas pudding

butter
leftover Christmas pudding,
    sliced or rolled into balls
cream or ice cream, to serve

HEAT A TABLESPOON OR SO of butter in a heavy-based pan. When hot, add the pudding and fry until crispy on the outside and warmed right through.

SERVE STRAIGHT AWAY with cream or ice cream.

Spiced bread and butter pudding

SERVES 6

We all buy too much food at Christmas, so here's a way of using up leftover bread or, in this case, stale croissants. The baking dish is set in a bain-marie, so the custard cooks to a blissful consistency — just softly set and wonderfully creamy.

4 large stale croissants
75 g unsalted butter,
    at room temperature
1 tsp ground mixed spice
1 tsp ground ginger
50 g sultanas
1 tbsp icing sugar, for dusting

For the custard
300 ml milk, at room
    temperature
300 ml double cream,
    at room temperature
1 vanilla pod, split
6 egg yolks
125 g caster sugar
single cream, to serve

PREHEAT THE OVEN TO 180°C/GAS 4. Butter a 1.7 litre shallow baking dish.

SLICE THE CROISSANTS THICKLY, then spread with the butter. Arrange the croissant slices in the prepared dish, butter-side up and overlapping, scattering in the mixed spice and sultanas as you do so.

TO MAKE THE CUSTARD, pour the milk and cream into a saucepan. Add the vanilla pod and place over a very low heat for about 5 minutes, until the mixture is almost boiling and well flavoured with vanilla.

MEANWHILE, in a large bowl, whisk together the egg yolks and caster sugar until light and foamy. Strain the flavoured milk onto the egg mixture, whisking all the time.

POUR THE EGG MIXTURE evenly over the croissants. Place the dish in a large roasting tin and pour in enough boiling water to come halfway up the sides of the dish. Bake in the oven for 45–50 minutes, until the custard is softly set and the top is crisp and golden.

REMOVE FROM THE OVEN and leave the pudding in the bain-marie until just warm. Sprinkle with the icing sugar and serve with cream.

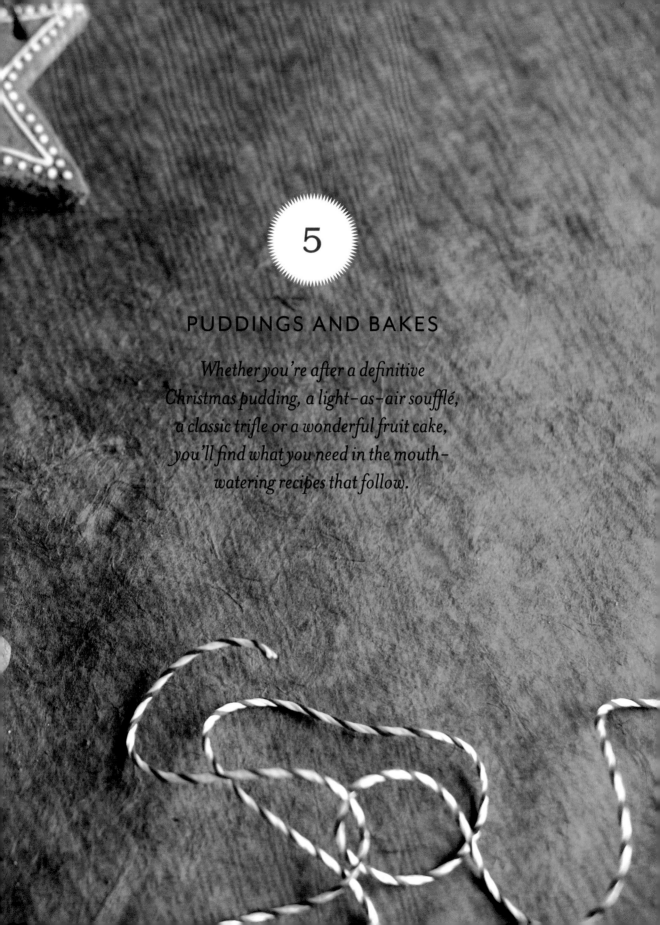

5

PUDDINGS AND BAKES

*Whether you're after a definitive
Christmas pudding, a light–as–air soufflé,
a classic trifle or a wonderful fruit cake,
you'll find what you need in the mouth-
watering recipes that follow.*

Christmas pudding

SERVES 8

Gordon's pudding mixture is fruity but lighter than the traditional one.

280 g suet
280 g golden caster sugar
280 g currants
280 g raisins
280 g sultanas
70 g chopped almonds
150 g plain flour
150 g fresh breadcrumbs
150 g good-quality mixed
   peel, chopped
60 ml lemon juice
1 tsp nutmeg
½ tsp salt
1 tbsp good-quality marmalade
3 eggs
180 ml Guinness
½ cooking apple, grated

PUT ALL THE INGREDIENTS in a large bowl and mix well, making sure that there are no pockets of flour or breadcrumbs.

BUTTER EIGHT 250 ML BOWLS or two 1 litre bowls. Divide the pudding mixture between them. Cut out circles of greaseproof paper and foil large enough to overlap the top of the bowls. Lay a foil circle over a paper one and make a pleat in the centre. Place over a pudding bowl and tie firmly around the rim with string. Do this with all the bowls.

PLACE THE BOWLS in a pan on a trivet or upturned saucer. Add boiling water to come a quarter of the way up the side of the puds, then cover and steam – 2 hours for little puds, 4–5 hours for large ones. Top up with water if you need to. The longer you steam the puddings the darker the mixture will get.

STEAM AGAIN for 1 hour before serving.

Brandy butter

Cream together 75 g unsalted butter with 75 g caster sugar or icing sugar. Gradually add 2–3 tbsp brandy, according to taste. If too strong, add a little boiling water. Finally, stir in the finely grated zest of half an orange.

Sticky date and orange pudding

SERVES 6

Wallow in glorious indulgence with this steaming hot dessert. Distinctly flavoured with oranges, dates and flecks of white chocolate, the light-textured spongy pudding is topped with a delicious toffee sauce. Serve with cream or custard.

175 g pitted dates
150 ml fresh orange juice
75 g unsalted butter, softened
150 g light muscovado sugar
2 eggs
150 g self-raising flour
25 g cocoa powder
½ tsp bicarbonate of soda
grated rind of 1 orange
50 g white chocolate,
    roughly chopped
pouring cream or custard,
    to serve

For the sauce
125 g light muscovado sugar
75 g unsalted butter
4 tbsp double cream
1 tbsp lemon juice

BUTTER A 1.4 LITRE PUDDING BOWL and line the base with a circle of greaseproof paper.

ROUGHLY CHOP THE DATES and place in a saucepan with the orange juice. Bring to the boil, lower the heat and simmer gently for 5 minutes. Leave to cool.

MEANWHILE PUT THE BUTTER, sugar and eggs in a large bowl. Sift in the flour, cocoa powder and bicarbonate of soda and beat well until evenly combined.

USING A SLOTTED SPOON, remove one-third of the date pieces from the saucepan and set aside. Add the dates and orange juice remaining in the pan to the pudding mixture, along with the orange rind and chocolate. Stir well, then turn into the prepared bowl.

COVER THE BOWL with a double thickness of greaseproof paper and a sheet of foil. Secure under the rim with string. Place in a steamer and add boiling water. Cover and steam for 2 hours. Top up with more boiling water as necessary during cooking.

MEANWHILE, MAKE THE SAUCE. Put the sugar, butter and cream into a small pan. Heat gently until the sugar dissolves, then stir in the reserved dates and the lemon juice. Boil for 1 minute.

REMOVE THE PUDDING from the steamer and invert onto a serving plate. Pour the hot toffee sauce over the pudding to coat evenly. Hand any remaining sauce around separately. Serve with pouring cream or custard.

Orange and cranberry mini puddings

MAKES 4

These little puddings can be eaten at any time of the year, but also make a delicious lower-fat alternative to traditional Christmas pudding.

25 g dried cranberries
1½ tsp golden syrup
115 g reduced-fat butter,
    plus extra for greasing,
    at room temperature
75 g caster sugar
2 eggs, lightly beaten
115 g self-raising flour
½ tsp baking powder
grated rind of 1 orange
150 ml orange juice

LIGHTLY BUTTER four mini pudding bowls (about 350 ml) and divide the cranberries between them. Top with the golden syrup and set aside.

CREAM THE BUTTER and caster sugar together until light and fluffy, then gradually add the eggs, a little at a time, beating between each addition. Fold in the flour, baking powder and orange rind until well combined, then stir in the orange juice.

PREPARE A STEAMER and bring the water in it to the boil.

DIVIDE THE PUDDING MIXTURE between the bowls and cover each one with a piece of foil. Cover the pan and steam over a medium heat for 40 minutes. Let the puddings stand for 5 minutes before uncovering and turning them onto serving plates.

IF NOT SERVING the puddings immediately, uncover them while they cool, then re-cover with clingfilm and keep in the fridge. To reheat, remove the clingfilm, cover with foil and steam, as above, for 18—20 minutes. Alternatively, microwave on Medium, covered with clingfilm, for 4 minutes.

Rum, raisin and white chocolate tart

SERVES 8

In this delicious tart, a layer of rum-soaked raisins is hidden beneath a spongy almond topping, which is heavily speckled with chunks of white chocolate. These melt to an irresistible fudge-like texture when the tart is served warm.

175 g raisins
6 tbsp rum
350 g white chocolate
50 g butter
125 g light muscovado sugar
2 eggs
125 g self-raising flour
25 g unblanched almonds,
   roughly chopped
icing sugar, for dusting

For the pastry
175 g plain white flour
pinch of salt
75 g unsalted butter,
   cut into small pieces
75 g caster sugar
3 egg yolks

PUT THE RAISINS in a bowl with the rum and leave overnight, or until most of the rum has been absorbed.

TO MAKE THE PASTRY, sift the flour and salt into a bowl. Rub in the butter using your fingertips until the mixture resembles fine breadcrumbs. Stir in the sugar and egg yolks, mixing to a smooth dough; if necessary, add 1 teaspoon cold water to bind it together. Knead lightly, wrap in clingfilm and chill for 30 minutes.

PREHEAT THE OVEN to 190°C/Gas 5. Meanwhile, roll out the pastry and use to line a 23 cm loose-bottomed flan tin. Line the pastry case with greaseproof paper or foil and fill with baking beans or dry rice. Bake in the oven for 15 minutes, then remove the beans/rice and lining and bake for 5–10 minutes longer, until the base is dry. Leave to cool. Lower the oven to 180°C/Gas 4.

MEANWHILE, chop 300 g of the chocolate into small pieces. Break up the remaining chocolate and put into a heatproof bowl set over a pan of simmering water. Add the butter and leave until melted.

BEAT THE SUGAR AND EGGS together in a bowl. Stir in the flour, melted chocolate and three-quarters of the chopped chocolate.

SPOON THE RAISINS and any rum into the pastry case. Pour in the chocolate mixture, then sprinkle with the remaining chocolate pieces and the almonds. Bake for about 40 minutes until just firm, covering the tart with foil about halfway through cooking to prevent it overbrowning. Serve warm, dusted with icing sugar. Crème fraîche is an ideal accompaniment.

GORDON RAMSAY

Pear tarte tatin

SERVES 8

Gordon adds a touch of spice to the ultimate French classic to create a welcome addition to the Christmas pudding repertoire.

8 ripe but firm pears
   (Comice are ideal)
100 g caster sugar
100 g butter
2 star anise
3 cardamom pods
1 large cinnamon stick
2 tbsp brandy
1 x 500 g block all-butter
   puff pastry

CORE THE PEARS, then peel as neatly as possible and halve. If you like, they can be prepared up to a day ahead and kept in the fridge, uncovered, so that they dry out.

TIP THE SUGAR, butter and spices into a 20 cm ovenproof frying pan and place over a high heat until bubbling. Shake the pan and stir the buttery sauce until it separates and the sugar caramelises to a toffee colour.

LAY THE PEARS IN THE SAUCE and cook for 10–12 minutes, turning, until completely caramelised. Don't worry about them burning – they won't – but you want to caramelise them as much as possible. Carefully add the brandy and let it flambé, then set the pears aside.

HEAT THE OVEN to 200°C/Gas 6. Meanwhile, roll out the pastry to the thickness of a £1 coin. Using a plate slightly larger than the top of the pan, cut out a circle, then press the edges of the circle to thin them out.

WHEN THE PEARS have cooled slightly, arrange them cut-side up in the pan. Rest the cinnamon stick on top in the centre, with the cardamom pods scattered around.

DRAPE THE PASTRY over the pears, then tuck the thinned edge down the side and under the fruit. Pierce the pastry a few times, then bake for 15 minutes. If a lot of juice bubbles up the side of the pan, carefully pour it off: this prevents the pastry becoming soggy when you later turn the tart out. Reduce the temperature to 180°C/Gas 4 and bake for 15 minutes more, until the pastry is golden. Leave the tart to stand for 10 minutes, then invert it carefully onto a serving dish.

Walnut and fig tart

SERVES 6

This is a gorgeous, dark treacly tart with a moist, sticky layer of figs encased in a crumbly pastry case — with walnuts adding a nutty crunch. To offset the sweetness of the tart, serve with crème fraîche.

150 g ready-to-eat dried figs
100 g fresh white breadcrumbs
90 ml molasses or dark treacle
135 ml golden syrup
2 tbsp lemon juice
125 g shelled walnuts

For the pastry
175 g plain flour
pinch of salt
125 g unsalted butter, in pieces
    at room temperature
2 egg yolks

FIRST MAKE THE PASTRY. Sift the flour and salt into a mound on a work surface. Make a well in the centre. Add the butter, egg yolks and 1 tablespoon cold water to the well. Using the fingertips of one hand, work the ingredients together to form a soft dough, adding a little extra water if necessary. Knead very lightly until smooth, then form into a flat round. Wrap in a plastic bag and chill for 30 minutes.

PREHEAT THE OVEN to 200°C/Gas 6.

ROLL OUT THE DOUGH on a lightly floured surface and use to line a 23 cm loose-bottomed flan tin. Prick the base with a fork and chill for 10 minutes.

MEANWHILE, trim the stems from the figs, then cut the fruit into small chunks. Set aside.

Put the breadcrumbs, molasses, golden syrup and lemon juice in a food processor or blender and whizz briefly until just combined. Add 75 g of the walnuts and whizz for just a few seconds until they are in rough chunks. (All the mixing and chopping can be done by hand if you prefer.)

LINE THE PASTRY CASE with greaseproof paper or foil and fill with baking beans or dry rice. Bake in the oven for 15 minutes, then remove the beans/rice and lining and bake for 5–10 minutes longer, until the base is dry.

SCATTER THE FIGS evenly inside the pastry case, then spoon the breadcrumb mixture over them. Arrange the reserved walnuts on top, pressing them down gently, and bake in the oven for 20–25 minutes, until the filling is just firm. Serve the tart warm, not hot, with crème fraîche.

Lemon thyme panna cotta with raspberry granita

SERVES 6

Change this recipe according to the season and you'll always have a make-ahead dinner party dessert with a wow factor.

2 gelatine leaves or 2 tsp powdered gelatine
600 ml double cream
150 ml full-fat milk
1 bunch lemon thyme (some supermarkets stock this)
100 g golden caster sugar
4 punnets raspberries
4 tbsp raspberry liqueur (e.g. Chambord)
3 tbsp icing sugar
white chocolate, for decoration (optional)

IF USING GELATINE LEAVES, soak in cold water until floppy. Bring the cream and milk to the boil, add the lemon thyme (saving a few leaves to add to the raspberries), then take off the heat and leave to infuse for 5 minutes.

NEXT YOU MUST ADD THE SUGAR and gelatine, but make sure you do it in the right order. If using soaked gelatine leaves, add the caster sugar to the hot cream mixture and stir until it dissolves. Then stir in the soaked gelatine, shaking off any excess water first. If using powdered gelatine, sprinkle it onto the cream mixture before the sugar, leave for a few seconds, then stir it in, add the sugar and stir that until it dissolves. Pour the lot through a fine sieve into a jug.

DIVIDE THE MIXTURE between six martini glasses, cover with clingfilm, put them on a tray and place in the fridge to set. If you don't put them on a tray, make sure they are level: the topping won't look as impressive on a sloping surface.

PUT 48 RASPBERRIES in a bowl with the liqueur and reserved lemon thyme leaves. You'll be using these whole, so don't squash them.

FOR THE GRANITA, put the remaining raspberries in another bowl with the icing sugar and 4 tablespoons water, cover tightly with clingfilm and put in a warm place (about 50–60°C) for an hour to encourage the raspberries to give up their juice.

[Continued overleaf]

DRAIN THE FRUIT through a fine sieve, gently pressing them to release their juice, into a freezer-proof container and freeze until solid. Stir once or twice while freezing if you want coarse crystals; if you leave it to freeze without stirring, the block will be more solid and you'll get a finer ice once you start scraping. You won't end up with a huge amount of liquid, so don't panic — you'll be scraping this into shavings of granita rather than serving it in big scoops.

TO SERVE, arrange 8 raspberries on top of each panna cotta. Standing them up neatly will make the dish look more impressive.

TAKE THE GRANITA out of the freezer and use a metal spoon to scrape the surface into shavings. Top each glass with a heap of shavings. Grate over some white chocolate if you want and serve straight away.

Blood orange and Cointreau sorbet

MAKES ABOUT 1 LITRE

A refreshingly tart, flame-coloured sorbet. Serve by itself, or layer in tall glass goblets with whipped cream flavoured with grated orange zest.

12–14 blood oranges
2 tbsp Cointreau or other
   orange-flavoured liqueur
2 tbsp sugar, or to taste

SQUEEZE AND STRAIN THE JUICE from the oranges. Add the liqueur and sugar, and stir until completely dissolved. Cover and chill for at least 2 hours. Churn and freeze in an ice cream maker. Once thickened, store in the freezer to harden. If you don't have an ice cream maker, put the mixture in a plastic container and freeze until half-frozen (about 1 hour). Remove and stir with a fork to break up the ice crystals. Return to the freezer and repeat this process twice more.

Pineapple and date salad with kumquats

SERVES 6

An ideal dessert to follow a rich festive dinner, this pretty fruit salad is made with seasonal oranges, kumquats, pineapple, fresh or dried dates and a sprinkling of walnuts. The kumquats are poached in an acacia honey syrup and acquire a wonderful musky flavour.

225 g kumquats
2 oranges
1 medium pineapple
12 fresh or dried dates
125 g walnut halves
whipped cream, to serve

For the syrup
75 ml acacia honey
50 g soft brown sugar
300 ml Earl Grey tea, strained

FIRST MAKE THE SYRUP. Place the honey, sugar and tea in a saucepan and bring to the boil. Boil for 1 minute.

HALVE THE KUMQUATS horizontally and place in the syrup. Simmer uncovered for about 10 minutes until the fruit is tender. Leave to cool in the syrup.

PEEL THE ORANGES as you would an apple, removing all the rind and white pith. Slice them crossways and place in a bowl. Using a sharp knife, cut the top and bottom off the pineapple and cut away the skin. Cut out the brown 'eyes'. Quarter the pineapple lengthways and cut out the core. Cut the flesh into large chunks. Carefully mix with the oranges.

HALVE THE DATES and remove the stones. Stir into the fruit mixture with the walnuts. Drain the kumquats and set aside; strain the syrup and pour over the fruit in the bowl. Cover and chill for 1 hour.

SPOON THE FRUIT SALAD into a serving dish or individual glass bowls and scatter the kumquats on top. Serve with whipped cream.

ANGELA HARTNETT

Figs in red wine

SERVES 4

There is a richness to this dessert that makes you just want to eat and eat. If you want to push the boat out, serve it with Zabaglione (page 173); if not, serve the figs with crème fraîche or a little double cream.

1 bottle good red wine, such as a Cabernet Sauvignon
500 ml ruby port
50 g sugar
12 ripe fresh figs

PLACE THE WINE and port in a pan with the sugar and bring to the boil. Allow to bubble until the liquid has reduced by half.

MEANWHILE, peel the figs. Add them to the reduced wine mixture and simmer over a low heat until they are a deep red colour, about 10 minutes. When they arc soft but not mushy — test by piercing with the tip of a knife — remove from the pan and place three figs in each serving dish.

RETURN THE POACHING LIQUOR to the heat and bring to the boil. Boil until it has reduced by two-thirds and formed a thick glaze. Pour the glaze over the figs and serve with the topping of your choice.

MICHEL
ROUX JR

Banana soufflé with crumble topping

SERVES 8

Light-as-air soufflé enfolds a luscious banana compote, and the topping provides a crunchy contrast.

3 bananas
1 tbsp light brown
    muscovado sugar
juice of 1 lemon
1 tbsp cornflour
2 tbsp dark rum
8 egg whites
80 g mixture of caster
    and icing sugar

For the compote
4 bananas
juice of 1 lemon
1 heaped tbsp demerara sugar
1 tbsp dark rum

For the crumble
1 tbsp rolled oats
1 tbsp desiccated coconut
1 tbsp chopped pistachios
1 tbsp chopped cashew nuts
1 tbsp demerara sugar

PEEL THE 3 BANANAS and put them in a pan with the brown sugar, lemon juice and 6 tablespoons water. Simmer for 5 minutes, squashing the bananas with the back of a fork, then transfer to a processor and purée.

DISSOLVE THE CORNFLOUR in the rum. Return the purée to the pan and whisk in the cornflour mixture over a high heat. Bring to the boil, cover and take off the heat.

TO MAKE THE COMPOTE, peel and slice the 4 bananas and put them in a pan with the lemon juice, sugar and rum. Cook over a moderate heat, mashing with the back of a fork until completely cooked and the consistency of compote. Cover and leave to cool.

HEAT THE OVEN to 190°C/Gas 5. Lightly butter eight 9 cm ramekins (6 cm deep), then dust with a little icing sugar.

WHISK THE EGG WHITES until frothy. Add the mixed sugars and continue to whisk until firm.

MIX ONE-THIRD of the egg whites with the banana purée until smooth. Lightly fold in the rest of the whites.

HALF-FILL THE RAMEKINS with the egg white mixture. Using two spoons, place equal numbers of compote quenelles on top. Cover with the rest of the whites and smooth the surface. Run the tip of a knife around the inside edge of the ramekins to help the mixture to rise evenly.

PLACE THE RAMEKINS in the oven for 4 minutes. Meanwhile, mix the crumble ingredients together. Sprinkle the crumble over the soufflés (this must be done quickly or the soufflés will collapse). Continue to cook for a further 4–5 minutes. The soufflés should be moist in the middle and slightly undercooked. Serve immediately.

Zabaglione

SERVES 6

If you're looking for a frothy dessert to follow a feast, look no further – zabaglione is rich, luscious and easy to make. Serve it with crisp biscuits, such as amaretti, or use it as a sauce to accompany other desserts, such as Figs in red wine (page 170).

PUT THE EGG YOLKS and sugar in a large bowl set over a pan of simmering water and beat with an electric whisk until smooth. Gradually whisk in the Marsala, then continue whisking for a further 10 minutes, or until the mixture has substantially increased in volume and is slightly foamy.

REMOVE THE BOWL from the pan and spoon the mixture into six serving glasses. Serve warm or cold with amaretti.

5 egg yolks
50 g caster sugar
150 ml Marsala

Lychee and coconut syllabub

SERVES 6

Syllabubs were originally served to cleanse and sharpen the palate, but this one is somewhat richer. A delicious soft coconut cream conceals a layer of luscious lychees. Canned ones will do at a pinch if fresh are not available. Alternatively, pineapple and rambutans make good alternatives.

75 g creamed coconut
150 ml sweet dessert wine, such as Moscatel de Valencia
a few tbsp preserved stem ginger in syrup
24 lychees, peeled if fresh
75 ml coconut liqueur, such as Malibu
450 ml double cream
coconut shreds, to decorate

GRATE THE COCONUT and place in a saucepan with the sweet wine and 3 tablespoons ginger syrup. Heat very gently until the coconut has melted; do not boil. Stir well and leave to cool.

CUT THE LYCHEES in half and remove the stones. Place in a bowl and pour over the coconut liqueur. Chop 2 tablespoons stem ginger and stir into the lychee mixture. Cover and chill for at least 30 minutes.

WHISK THE CREAM until it holds soft peaks. Gently fold in the coconut and wine mixture – it should hold its shape; if it is a little runny, whisk lightly until it thickens.

DIVIDE THE LYCHEES and liqueur between six tall glasses. Spoon over the coconut cream syllabub, then chill for at least 30 minutes before serving.

FOR THE DECORATION, toast some of the coconut shreds. Arrange the plain and toasted coconut shreds on the syllabubs to serve.

MICHEL
ROUX SR

Ginger crème brûlée

SERVES 6—8

In its classic form, crème brûlée is on the rich side, but this version is fresh-tasting and easy to digest, thanks to the ginger.

80 g very fresh root ginger
500 ml milk
500 ml whipping cream
150 g caster sugar
200 g egg yolks (about 10 eggs)
70 g demerara sugar
80 g stem ginger in syrup,
    cut into small dice

PREHEAT THE OVEN to 100°C/Gas ¼.

PEEL THE ROOT GINGER, grate it finely, then transfer to a square of muslin and squeeze out as much juice as possible into a small jug or dish.

PUT THE MILK, cream and 90 g of the caster sugar into a pan and heat, stirring regularly with a balloon whisk, until the mixture is homogeneous, then bring slowly to the boil. Meanwhile, put the egg yolks into a bowl with the remaining caster sugar and lightly whisk.

AS SOON AS THE MILK and cream mixture reaches the boil, pour it a little at a time over the egg yolks, whisking all the time, then add the ginger juice. Divide the mixture between 15 cm gratin dishes and place them on a baking sheet. Transfer to the oven and cook for 30 minutes, or until set. Transfer the dishes to a cooling rack and leave to cool at room temperature, then refrigerate until ready to serve.

JUST BEFORE YOU ARE READY TO SERVE, sprinkle the demerara sugar over the crème brûlées and caramelise, either by using a kitchen blowtorch or placing them under a very hot grill, until a fine, pale, nut-brown crust develops. Place the preserved ginger dice on top of each crème brûlée and serve at once.

Raspberry and almond trifle

SERVES 6

An unusual trifle of ratafias and toasted almonds soaked in an almond liqueur, covered with fresh or frozen raspberries, then topped with a rich syllabub flavoured with Madeira and almond liqueur. For a less alcoholic version, omit sprinkling the ratafias with liqueur.

125 g blanched almonds
450 g fresh or frozen raspberries
juice and finely grated rind
    of 1 lemon
icing sugar, to taste
225 g ratafias
5 tbsp Amaretto di Saronno,
    or other almond liqueur
150 ml dry Madeira or sherry
freshly grated nutmeg
450 ml double cream

PLACE THE ALMONDS on a tray and toast under the grill or in a moderate oven until evenly golden. Allow to cool, then chop roughly.

PURÉE HALF THE RASPBERRIES in a blender or food processor. Sieve to remove the pips, then stir in the lemon juice and icing sugar to taste.

CRUMBLE THE RATAFIAS, setting a few aside for later, and divide between individual serving glasses. Sprinkle with all but 1 tablespoon of the toasted almonds and 3 tablespoons Amaretto. (If preferred, the trifle can be assembled in one large serving dish.) Scatter in the whole raspberries and sprinkle with a little icing sugar. Pour in raspberry purée, then cover and chill in the refrigerator.

MEANWHILE, put the lemon rind in a bowl with the Madeira, the remaining Amaretto and some nutmeg. Leave to macerate for at least 1 hour, then strain.

WHISK THE CREAM with icing sugar to taste until just beginning to thicken, then gradually whisk in the flavoured wine and liqueur until the mixture holds soft peaks. Spoon over the raspberries and ratafias. Cover and chill for at least 1 hour.

JUST BEFORE SERVING, decorate with the reserved ratafias and toasted almonds.

ANGELA HARTNETT

Tiramisu

SERVES 6—8

I'm willing to bet that anybody who dined out in the UK in the 1980s will have had a bad tiramisu experience. It was invariably served up in a big slab with heavy sponge and too much booze. But made properly, it's very good indeed. My Auntie Maria gave me this recipe: the secret is to make sure that the coffee is strong and the liqueur cuts through the sweetness.

4 eggs, separated
75 g caster sugar
100 g mascarpone
1 vanilla pod, split lengthways
    and seeds scraped out
200 ml espresso coffee
25—50 ml brandy (depending
    how boozy you like it)
12 sponge fingers
cocoa powder, to dust

USING AN ELECTRIC MIXER, cream the egg yolks and sugar together until pale and fluffy. Add the mascarpone and vanilla seeds and whisk together to combine.

IN A SEPARATE BOWL, whisk the egg whites until they form stiff peaks, then fold them into the mascarpone mixture.

MIX THE COFFEE and brandy in a shallow dish. Dip the sponge fingers into the liquid and use them to line the base of a serving dish or individual glasses. Spoon the mascarpone mixture over the sponge, then dust the top with cocoa powder to finish. Refrigerate for at least 8 hours (ideally overnight) to chill thoroughly before serving. This allows the flavours to develop.

Christmas ice cream

MAKES ABOUT 1 LITRE

Packed with nuts and plump dried fruit, this deliciously creamy ice is an excellent alternative to Christmas pudding. Start the recipe the day before to allow time for soaking the fruit.

25 g dried cranberries
25 g mixed raisins and sultanas
55 g finely chopped mixed peel
100 ml Marsala, rum or brandy
200 ml whipping cream
250 ml cold vanilla custard
  (good-quality ready-made
  custard is fine)
40 g macadamia nuts, chopped
40 g amaretti biscuits, crumbled

PUT THE DRIED FRUIT and mixed peel in a bowl. Add the Marsala and leave to soak for 24 hours.

LIGHTLY WHIP THE CREAM until the beaters leave a faint trail when lifted from the cream. Drain the soaked fruits and stir into the cream, along with the custard. Cover and chill for at least 2 hours.

ADD THE NUTS and crumbled amaretti. Churn and freeze in an ice cream maker. Once thickened, either serve right away, or store in the freezer to harden. If you don't have an ice cream maker, put the mixture in a plastic container and freeze until half-frozen (about 1 hour). Remove and stir with a fork to break up the ice crystals. Return to the freezer and repeat this process twice more.

Christmas morning muffins

MAKES 12

Moist muffins bursting with cranberries make a wonderful start to the celebrations. Have all the dry ingredients mixed together, and prepare the muffin tin the night before. On Christmas morning, just stir in the liquids and cranberries, fill the tins and bake. Serve from the oven — these muffins do not reheat well.

175 g fresh cranberries
50 g icing sugar, sifted
150 g plain wholemeal flour
150 g plain white flour
1 tbsp baking powder
1 tsp ground mixed spice
1 tsp salt
50 g soft light brown sugar
1 egg
250 ml milk
60 ml vegetable oil
crème fraîche, to serve
   (optional)

PREHEAT THE OVEN to 180°C/Gas 4. Line a 12-hole muffin tin with paper cases or simply grease with butter.

HALVE THE CRANBERRIES and place in a bowl with the icing sugar. Toss gently to mix.

SIFT TOGETHER THE FLOURS, baking powder, mixed spice, salt and soft brown sugar into a large bowl. Make a well in the centre.

BEAT THE EGG with the milk and oil. Add to the dry ingredients and stir just until blended, then lightly and quickly stir in the cranberries. The mixture should look roughly mixed, with lumps and floury pockets.

FILL EACH MUFFIN HOLE two-thirds full with the mixture. Bake in the oven for about 20 minutes, or until well risen and golden brown.

TRANSFER THE MUFFINS to a wire rack to cool slightly. Serve while still warm, with crème fraîche if desired.

Luxury Christmas cake

MAKES 30—40 SLICES

Make this cake any time from mid-November to mid-December. Store tightly wrapped to prevent the cake from drying out; spear occasionally with a skewer and 'feed' with brandy.

1 lemon

1 orange

225 g dried apricots

175 g pitted prunes

225 g currants

125 g sultanas

225 g raisins

150 ml brandy, rum, porter or sweet stout

175 g glacé cherries

175 g unblanched almonds

125 g chopped candied peel

350 g self-raising white flour

2 tsp mixed spice

1 tsp salt

300 g unsalted butter, softened

300 g soft dark muscovado sugar

6 eggs, beaten

4 tbsp treacle

GRATE THE RIND from the lemon and orange and squeeze the juice. Roughly chop the apricots and prunes. Mix them together with the citrus rinds and juices in a large bowl, along with the currants, sultanas and raisins. Add the brandy, cover and leave to macerate overnight, stirring occasionally.

THE NEXT DAY, preheat the oven to 160°C/Gas 3. Line a 25 cm round cake tin, or 23 cm square one, with a double or triple layer of greaseproof paper. Grease with butter.

WASH, DRY AND HALVE THE CHERRIES. Roughly chop the almonds. Add the cherries, nuts and candied peel to the macerated fruit mixture and stir well.

SIFT THE FLOUR, spice and salt together. In a large bowl, cream together the butter and sugar until fluffy. Gradually mix in the eggs, beating well between each addition to prevent curdling. Stir in the treacle, then fold in the flour and fruit mixtures.

SPOON THE MIXTURE into the prepared tin, level the surface, then make a slight hollow in the middle. Bake for 1 hour, then lower the temperature to 140°C/Gas 1 and bake for a further 2—3 hours. Cover the top of the cake with buttered paper if it's browning too much. Test for readiness by inserting a skewer into the centre of the cake — if it comes out clean, the cake is done.

LEAVE IN THE TIN until cool enough to handle, then turn out onto a wire rack to cool completely in the paper. When cold, keep one layer of greaseproof paper on the cake, then wrap in foil. Store in a cool dry place. The cake can be decorated up to one week before Christmas.

Iced gingerbread with stem ginger

MAKES 16 SQUARES

Gingerbread is said to be one of the oldest forms of cake in the world. Most European countries have their own version. One of the major advantages of homemade gingerbread is that it improves with keeping.

100 g softened butter
100 g light muscovado sugar
2 large eggs
150 g black treacle
150 g golden syrup
225 g plain flour
1 tsp ground ginger
1 tsp ground mixed spice
½ teaspoon bicarbonate of soda
2 tbsp milk

For the icing
175 g icing sugar
3 tbsp stem ginger syrup
about 3 tsp water
2.5 cm piece stem ginger

PREHEAT THE OVEN to 160°C/Gas 3. Grease an 18 cm deep square cake tin and line the bottom with baking parchment.

MEASURE THE BUTTER, sugar, eggs, treacle and golden syrup into a bowl and beat until thoroughly mixed. Sift the flour with the spices and fold into the mixture. Add the bicarbonate of soda to the milk and stir this into the mixture. Pour into the prepared tin and bake for 1 hour.

LOWER THE OVEN TEMPERATURE to 150°C/Gas 2 and bake for a further 15–30 minutes, until well risen and firm to the touch. Leave to cool in the tin for 10 minutes, then turn out, peel off the parchment and finish cooling on a wire rack.

FOR THE ICING, sift the icing sugar into a bowl and add the stem ginger syrup and a teaspoon or so of water to make a smooth spreading consistency. Finely chop the stem ginger and add to the icing. Pour the icing over the cake and leave to set before cutting into 16 squares.

MARY BERRY

Cranberry and apricot fruit cake

This cake is robust enough to pack for a picnic and also makes a good alternative Christmas cake. Instead of dried cranberries, you can use the same weight of red or natural quartered glacé cherries, but wash and dry them thoroughly.

1 x 227 g tin pineapple in natural juice
350 g ready-to-eat dried apricots
150 g whole blanched almonds
350 g dried cranberries
75 g ground almonds
350 g sultanas
finely grated rind of 2 lemons
250 g self-raising flour
250 g caster sugar
250 g softened butter
5 large eggs

PREHEAT THE OVEN to 150°C/Gas 2. Grease a 23 cm deep round cake tin, then line the bottom and sides with baking parchment.

DRAIN THE PINEAPPLE, discarding the juice. Coarsely chop, then dry thoroughly on kitchen paper. Snip the apricots into pieces and coarsely chop 100 g of the almonds. Combine all the fruits, the chopped and ground nuts and the lemon rind in a large bowl and mix well.

PUT THE FLOUR, sugar, butter and eggs into a large mixing bowl and beat until smooth. Fold in the fruit mixture, then spoon into the prepared tin. Level the top with the back of a spoon and decorate with the remaining blanched almonds, arranging them in concentric circles.

BAKE FOR ABOUT 2½ hours, or until the cake is nicely browned. If it shows signs of becoming too browned before it is cooked, cover the top loosely with foil. When cooked, the cake should show signs of shrinking away from the side of the tin and a skewer inserted into the centre of the cake should come out clean. Leave to cool in the tin for about 30 minutes, then turn out and finish cooling on a wire rack, leaving the parchment in place.

New Year tipsy cake

SERVES 8—10

A 'tipsy' cake seems appropriate for a New Year celebration. The cake is filled and topped with orange segments, but can also be made with various fruits. Potato flour is available from health-food shops and good delicatessens.

5 large eggs, 2 of them
    separated
275 g caster sugar
65 g sifted self-raising flour
65 g sifted potato flour (fécule)
    or cornflour
grated rind of 1 lemon

For the sugar syrup
50 g granulated sugar
150 ml sweet white wine
1 tbsp brandy

For the filling and decoration
225 g orange segments
450 ml whipping or double
    cream, whipped
1 orange, thinly sliced

PREHEAT THE OVEN to 180°C/Gas 4. Grease a 23 cm deep round cake tin; line the bottom with parchment.

PUT THE 3 WHOLE EGGS, the 2 egg yolks and the sugar into a large bowl and beat over hot water until thick and mousse-like, and the mixture leaves a trail when the whisk is lifted.

IN A SEPARATE BOWL, whisk the egg whites until stiff but not dry and fold into the yolk mixture, along with the flours and lemon rind. Turn into the prepared tin and bake for about 45—50 minutes, or until the cake is well risen and golden, and the surface springs back when lightly pressed with a fingertip. Leave to cool in the tin for 10 minutes, then turn out, peel off the parchment and finish cooling on a wire rack.

IN A SMALL PAN, gently dissolve the granulated sugar in 3 tablespoons water over a low heat. Bring the syrup to the boil and allow to boil for 2 minutes. Set aside to cool, then add the wine and brandy.

WHEN THE CAKE IS COLD, use a serrated knife to make a cut around the top of the cake about 2.5 cm in from the edge and about 4 cm deep. Insert the knife in the cut, then hold it almost horizontal and cut towards the centre of the cake. The idea is to remove a 'lid' of sponge, leaving a flan case shape. Put the lid aside.

SOAK THE CAKE with two-thirds of the sugar syrup and fill with the orange segments and half the whipped cream. Replace the lid and moisten with the remaining syrup. Smooth the remaining cream over the top and sides of the cake and decorate with the slices of orange.

MARY
BERRY

Ultimate chocolate roulade

SERVES 8–10

Always popular, this roulade freezes very well. Raspberries (frozen are fine) can be added to the filling if you wish. For a special occasion, scatter masses of fresh raspberries around the roulade on the serving platter — it looks stunning.

175 g plain chocolate, broken into pieces
175 g caster sugar
6 eggs, separated
2 tbsp cocoa powder, sifted
300 ml double cream
icing sugar

LIGHTLY GREASE a 33 x 23 cm Swiss roll tin and line with baking parchment, pushing it into the corners. Preheat the oven to 180°C/Gas 4.

MELT THE CHOCOLATE in a bowl placed over a pan of hot water, stirring occasionally. Allow to cool slightly.

PUT THE SUGAR and egg yolks into a bowl and whisk on a high speed until light and creamy. Add the cooled chocolate and stir until evenly blended.

WHISK THE EGG WHITES in a large mixing bowl until stiff but not dry. Stir a large spoonful of the egg whites into the chocolate mixture, mix gently, then fold in the remaining egg whites, followed by the cocoa powder. Turn the mixture into the prepared tin and gently level the surface. Bake for about 20 minutes, until firm.

REMOVE THE CAKE from the oven, leave in the tin and place a cooling rack over the cake. Place a clean, damp tea towel over the rack and leave for several hours or overnight in a cool place; the cake will sink slightly. (If the tea towel dries out, simply re-dampen it.)

WHIP THE CREAM until it just holds its shape. Dust a large piece of non-stick baking parchment with icing sugar. Turn the roulade out onto the parchment and peel off the lining paper. Spread the cake with the whipped cream, then roll up, starting with one of the short edges; roll tightly to begin with and use the paper to help. Don't worry if the sponge cracks — that is quite normal and part of the roulade's charm. Dust with icing sugar before serving.

Cranberry mince pies

MAKES 12

A seasonal variation on a Christmas classic, these pies provide the finishing touch to your celebration feast.

250 g '00' flour or plain flour, plus extra for rolling out
25 g icing sugar
125 g butter, chilled and cubed
finely grated zest of 1 orange or lemon
1 medium egg, beaten
200 g luxury mincemeat
1 x 75 g packet dried cranberries
1 egg yolk, beaten with 1 tsp water, to glaze
icing sugar, to serve

WHIZZ TOGETHER the flour, icing sugar and butter until they form fine crumbs. With the blades running, add the zest, then the egg, and process for a few seconds, until the mixture forms clumps. If you need to, work in a few trickles of ice-cold water, but for the shortest pastry, try to avoid this if you can.

TIP ONTO a very lightly floured surface, knead briefly until smooth, then chill in the fridge for 30 minutes, or until firm. The pastry can be made up to 3 days ahead or frozen for up to a month.

LIGHTLY DUST the work surface with flour, then roll out the pastry to the thickness of a £1 coin. Cut out 12 x 8 cm rounds with a fluted cutter and press into a 12-hole non-stick bun tin. Reroll the trimmings to the same thickness and use a 5 cm star-shaped cutter to stamp out 12 lids.

SPOON ABOUT 2 teaspoons mincemeat into each pastry case, sprinkle with cranberries, then press on the lids. The pies can be frozen for up to 1 month at this point. If you want to bake them now, chill for 20 minutes while you heat the oven to 190°C/Gas 5.

BRUSH THE TOPS with the egg-wash, then bake for 15–20 minutes, until golden and crisp. Cool for a few minutes, then lever out of the tins with a table knife and cool on a wire rack. Store in an airtight container for up to 1 week. Warm gently to serve, dusted with sifted icing sugar.

Christmas biscuits

MAKES 20—25

Spicy gingerbread is a lovely teatime treat, but it can be extra fun if you make Christmas tree decorations from it too. Simply stamp out stars, trees, holly leaves and so on, using suitable cutters, and make a small hole in the top of each one for a ribbon to be threaded through after baking so they can be hung on the tree.

350 g white flour
1 tsp bicarbonate of soda
2 tbsp ground ginger
1 tbsp ground cinnamon
½ tsp ground cloves
125 g butter
175 g soft light brown sugar
2 tbsp golden syrup
1 egg (size 4)

To finish
lustre powder
icing
narrow ribbon

LINE TWO BAKING SHEETS with non-stick baking parchment. Preheat the oven to 190°C/Gas 5.

SIFT THE FLOUR with the bicarbonate of soda and spices into a large bowl. Rub in the butter until the mixture resembles fine breadcrumbs. Stir in the sugar.

WARM THE GOLDEN SYRUP very slightly and beat in the egg. Cool slightly, then pour onto the flour mixture. Beat to a soft dough using a wooden spoon. Bring together with your hands and knead until smooth.

ON A LIGHTLY FLOURED SURFACE, roll out the dough to a 5 mm thickness. Stamp out your chosen shapes and make a hole in each one with the point of a skewer. Transfer to the baking sheets and chill for 15 minutes.

BAKE THE GINGERBREAD SHAPES for 8—10 minutes, or until golden brown. Leave to cool and harden for 10 minutes on the baking sheet, then transfer to a wire rack to cool completely.

DECORATE THE SHAPES with lustre powder and coloured icing if you like. Allow to dry before threading with ribbon and hanging from the tree.

Florentines

MAKES 12

These enticing chewy morsels are rich with fruit and nuts, and this version also includes sunflower seeds. After baking, the edges of the florentines are rolled in melted chocolate.

60 g unsalted butter
50 g caster sugar
2 tbsp double cream
25 g sunflower seeds
20 g chopped mixed peel
20 g sultanas
25 g glacé cherries
40 g flaked almonds
15 g plain flour
125 g dark chocolate,
    broken into pieces

PREHEAT THE OVEN to 180°C/Gas 4. Lightly grease a large baking sheet.

MELT THE BUTTER in a small saucepan. Add the sugar and heat gently until dissolved, then bring to the boil. Remove from the heat and stir in the cream, sunflower seeds, mixed peel, sultanas, cherries, almonds and flour. Beat well until evenly combined.

PLACE HEAPED TEASPOONFULS of the mixture on the baking sheet, spacing them well apart to allow room for spreading. (You'll probably need to cook half the mixture at a time.)

BAKE FOR ABOUT 6–8 minutes, until the biscuits have spread considerably and the edges are golden brown. Remove from the oven and, working quickly, use a large, plain metal biscuit cutter to push the edges towards the centre to neaten. Finish by rotating the cutter around each biscuit to make them perfectly round. Return to the oven for a further 2 minutes or until deep golden.

LEAVE THE FLORENTINES on the baking sheet for 2 minutes to cool slightly, then transfer to a wire rack to cool completely. Bake the remaining mixture in the same way.

MELT THE CHOCOLATE in a heatproof bowl over a pan of simmering water. Stir until smooth. Roll the edges of the biscuits in the chocolate and place on a sheet of baking parchment until set. Store in an airtight tin.

6

PARTY FOOD AND DRINKS

*Dazzle your guests with some exciting
recipes for party nibbles and drinks — from
tiger prawn blinis and asparagus frittata
to blueberry martinis and mango mojitos.
A delicious time will be had by all.*

Roasted nuts in rosemary and butter

SERVES 4—6

I pinched this recipe from the Union Square Café in New York, where they serve these nuts at the bar. As soon as you walk in, you can smell the delicious herby aroma. Although cooked in butter, the nuts are not at all greasy — just lightly coated, sweet and aromatic.

500 g mixed nuts
250 g butter
pinch of cayenne pepper
pinch of paprika
½ bunch fresh rosemary, chopped
50 g soft light brown sugar
salt

IN A PAN large enough to hold all the nuts in a single layer, melt the butter over a high heat until it starts to foam. Add the nuts and immediately lower the heat to medium. Shake the pan constantly so that the nuts colour all over. Once they have browned, about 3 minutes, add the cayenne, paprika and rosemary, together with a little salt. Mix well and sprinkle in the brown sugar.

REMOVE FROM THE HEAT, check the seasoning and drain through a colander. Allow to cool, then serve in bowls with a little more salt sprinkled on top.

Bruschette with asparagus, rocket and Parma ham

MAKES 4

A classic Italian bruschetta is simply grilled bread rubbed with garlic and drizzled with olive oil. It can, of course, be topped with all sorts of combinations, as suggested below.

225 g asparagus
50 ml extra virgin olive oil
4 large thick slices rustic bread
1 garlic clove, halved
50 g rocket
4 slices Parma ham
shavings of Parmesan cheese,
    to serve

For the dressing
scant 2 tbsp extra virgin olive oil
1 tsp lemon juice
½ tsp thin honey
salt and freshly ground pepper

PREHEAT THE OVEN to its lowest setting and preheat the grill.

TRIM THE WOODY ENDS of the asparagus and peel the lower ends of the stalks to remove any tough stringy parts if necessary. Brush with a little of the oil and grill for 4–5 minutes, turning frequently, until the spears are charred and tender. Transfer to a small warmed dish and keep warm in the oven.

TOAST THE BREAD LIGHTLY on both sides and rub all over with garlic. Drizzle liberally with olive oil and keep warm in the oven with the asparagus.

PLACE THE ROCKET in a small bowl. Put the dressing ingredients in a screw-topped jar and shake vigorously to combine. Pour the dressing over the rocket and toss to coat all the leaves.

REMOVE THE ASPARAGUS and bread from the oven. Arrange the bruschette on a platter and top each slice with a handful of the dressed rocket leaves, a few asparagus spears and a slice of Parma ham. Top with shavings of Parmesan and serve at once, drizzled with a little extra olive oil if wished.

Topping ideas
• Artichokes and Parma ham
• Chicken liver pâté and sliced olive
• Goats' cheese and cherry tomato
• Mozzarella and anchovies/chillies/olives
• Peperonata (page 129)
• Prosciutto and tomato
• Asparagus and Parmesan

Asparagus, broad bean and Parmesan frittata

MAKES ABOUT 16 PIECES

An Italian omelette might not seem like party food, but it's ideal if cut into bite-sized pieces. It's cooked slowly over a low heat and the filling can either be stirred into the eggs or scattered over the top; sometimes it is finished off under the grill. A frittata is served perfectly set, never folded.

175 g small new potatoes
225 g asparagus
225 g frozen broad beans, thawed
6 eggs
50 g freshly grated Parmesan cheese
3 tbsp chopped mixed fresh herbs, such as parsley, oregano and thyme
50 g butter
salt and freshly ground pepper

Variation

Lay 4 slices of prosciutto over the top of the lightly set frittata and grill for 2–3 minutes, until crisp.

COOK THE POTATOES in boiling salted water for 15–20 minutes, until tender. Allow to cool, then slice thickly.

MEANWHILE, trim the asparagus, removing any woody parts of the stems. Steam for 12 minutes until tender, then plunge into cold water to set the colour and cool completely.

SLIP THE BROAD BEANS out of their waxy skins. Drain the asparagus, pat dry, then cut into short lengths. Mix with the broad beans.

PUT THE EGGS in a bowl with a good pinch of salt, plenty of pepper and half the Parmesan. Beat thoroughly until evenly blended, then stir in the asparagus, broad beans and chopped herbs.

MELT 40 G OF THE BUTTER in a 25 cm non-stick, heavy-based frying pan. When foaming, pour in the egg mixture. Turn down the heat to as low as possible. Cook for about 15 minutes, until the frittata is set and the top is still a little runny.

PREHEAT THE GRILL. Scatter the cooked potato over the frittata and sprinkle with the remaining Parmesan. Dot with the rest of the butter. Place under the hot grill to lightly brown the cheese and just set the top; don't allow it to brown too much or it will dry out.

SLIDE THE FRITTATA onto a warmed dish and cut into wedges to serve.

Tiger prawn blinis with wasabi and horseradish sauce

MAKES 16

Ideal for a party, these little blinis look stunning and taste wonderful.

1 medium avocado
juice of ½ lemon
1 tbsp light cream cheese
1 tsp Japanese wasabi
1 tsp Mary Berry's
   Horseradish Sauce
sea salt
16 fresh blinis
16 tiger king prawns,
   shelled and cooked
fresh dill, to garnish

PREHEAT THE OVEN to 180°C/Gas 4.

STONE AND PEEL the avocado, then gently mash the flesh with a fork until smooth. Add the lemon juice, cream cheese, wasabi and horseradish sauce, and mix together to form a paste, but still with a bit of texture. Season with a little salt.

PLACE THE BLINIS in the oven for 3–5 minutes to warm through.

ARRANGE THE BLINIS on a platter. Carefully spoon a little of the avocado mixture onto each one. Arrange a tiger prawn on top and garnish with a sprig of dill.

Prawn, chorizo and tomato kebabs

MAKES 12

Perfect party food — a fantastic combination of flavours, all contained in one bite-sized hot canapé.

6 cherry tomatoes, halved
2 garlic cloves, thinly sliced
2 thyme sprigs, broken
　　into small pieces
olive oil
salt
12 slices chorizo from a
　　whole sausage
12 raw tiger prawns,
　　peeled and heads removed
12 basil leaves, cut in half

HEAT THE OVEN to 180°C/Gas 4. Put the tomatoes cut-side up on a baking sheet and top each one with a slice of garlic, a piece of thyme, a drizzle of olive oil and a sprinkling of salt. Cook for 30 minutes.

GRILL THE CHORIZO and fry the prawns in a little oil, keeping everything warm. When the tomatoes are done, take 12 skewers and push a prawn, a piece of basil, a piece of chorizo, some more basil and a tomato half onto each one.

Prawn rolls

SERVES 4

Here raw prawns are rolled in thin strips of filo pastry and deep-fried until crisp and golden. These traditional Thai snacks, with the prawn tails protruding cheekily from the pastry, are fun to make and eat. They are served with a sweet and sour dipping sauce.

2 spring onions, trimmed
1 garlic clove, peeled
1 tsp salt
1 tsp grated fresh root ginger
1 tsp Thai red curry paste
1 tbsp chopped fresh coriander
1 tsp tamarind paste
½ tsp sugar
16 large raw tiger prawns
4–8 sheets filo pastry
1 egg white, beaten
vegetable oil, for deep-frying

For the dipping sauce
2 small red chillies
50 g caster sugar
50 ml rice vinegar
½ tsp salt

Tip
Thai curry paste and tamarind paste can both be bought from supermarkets.

START BY MAKING THE DIPPING SAUCE. Finely chop the chillies, discarding the seeds if preferred. Place in a small pan with the sugar, vinegar, salt and 2 tablespoons water. Bring slowly to the boil, stirring until the sugar has dissolved, then remove from the heat and set aside to cool.

ROUGHLY CHOP THE SPRING ONIONS and garlic. Using a spice grinder or pestle and mortar, grind the salt, ginger, curry paste and coriander to a smooth paste. Stir in the tamarind paste and sugar.

CUT THE HEADS OFF THE PRAWNS, then peel away the shells. Make a slit down the back of each prawn and remove the dark intestinal vein. Rinse well and pat dry.

CUT THE FILO PASTRY into 16 strips, each 7.5 cm wide and 15 cm long. Keep covered with a lightly dampened tea towel.

WORKING WITH ONE STRIP OF PASTRY at a time, brush lightly with a little egg white. Spread 1 teaspoon of the spice mixture at one end of the strip, top with a prawn and roll the pastry up to enclose all but the tail. Repeat to make 16 rolls.

HEAT A 10 CM DEPTH OF OIL in a deep, heavy-based saucepan to 180°C, or until a cube of bread dropped into the oil browns in 30 seconds. Fry batches of the prawn rolls in the hot oil for 2–3 minutes, until crisp and golden. Drain on kitchen paper and serve hot with the dipping sauce.

Warm turkey, Brie and cranberry wraps

MAKES AS MANY AS YOU HAVE LEFTOVERS

These wraps make lovely party nibbles if sliced into smallish pieces.

soft flour tortillas
leftover turkey
slices of Brie or Camembert
cranberry sauce
watercress
melted butter

PREHEAT THE OVEN to 220°C/Gas 7.

ARRANGE A FEW TORTILLAS on a work surface. Place some turkey and slices of cheese on each one, top with a few spoonfuls of cranberry sauce and a scattering of watercress. Roll into a wrap, brush with butter and place on a baking tray. Heat in the oven for 10 minutes.

CUT IN HALF on the angle and serve with potato crisps as part of a buffet.

ANGELA HARTNETT

Baby peppers stuffed with goats' cheese

SERVES 3—4

This is actually a Spanish tapas dish, which is usually served as a snack with drinks. The peppers make great party nibbles for vegetarians.

200 g sweet baby peppers
1 tbsp olive oil
150 g soft goats' cheese
1 pinch finely chopped fresh rosemary
½ tsp finely chopped fresh flatleaf parsley
½ tsp finely chopped fresh basil
salt and freshly ground pepper

PREHEAT THE OVEN to 200°C/Gas 6.

CUT THE PEPPERS in half with a sharp knife, keeping the green stem attached. Remove the seeds and white core. Place the peppers on a baking sheet and drizzle with the olive oil. Season and bake in the oven for about 5 minutes, or until soft. Remove from the oven and allow to cool.

COMBINE THE GOATS' CHEESE and herbs in a bowl and check the seasoning. Spoon the filling into the pepper halves. (They can be prepared up to this stage in advance and set aside until needed.)

RETURN THE PEPPERS to the oven for 2—3 minutes to warm through the filling, then serve straight away.

Bittersweet chocolate nut slice

MAKES 30 SLICES

An indulgent treat for chocolate lovers. Lightly speckled with toasted almonds, stem ginger and raisins, and subtly flavoured with brandy, bitter chocolate can be relished in virtually unadulterated bliss. Once made, the roll can be refrigerated for up to a week, ready to be thinly sliced as required.

40 g blanched almonds, finely chopped
100 g bitter chocolate, broken into pieces
40 g unsalted butter
15 g stem ginger, finely diced
25 g raisins, preferably Lexia (extra large Muscatel raisins), roughly chopped
2 tbsp brandy

For the decoration
75 g flaked almonds
75 g white chocolate

Variation

For a sweeter alternative, use milk or white chocolate rather than plain.

PREHEAT THE GRILL, then lightly toast the almonds. Place the chocolate in a heatproof bowl set over a pan of simmering water. Add the butter and leave until melted.

ADD THE TOASTED ALMONDS, ginger, raisins and brandy to the melted chocolate and stir gently until evenly mixed.

LAY A SHEET OF GREASEPROOF PAPER on the work surface and spoon the chocolate mixture across the centre. Roll the chocolate into a cylinder about 3 cm wide, using the greaseproof paper to help you. Fold under the ends of the paper. Chill the roll in the refrigerator for 2 hours, or until firm.

MEANWHILE, crush the flaked almonds into slightly smaller pieces, then lightly toast them. Break up the white chocolate and melt in a heatproof bowl set over a pan of simmering water.

UNWRAP THE CHOCOLATE ROLL. Using a palette knife, quickly spread the white chocolate all over the surface of the log, then roll in the almonds until evenly covered. Chill for a further 1 hour, until set. Serve cut into thin slices.

Mulled wine

SERVES 6—8

Of all the drinks consumed at Christmas, mulled wine is probably the best known and most traditional. This simple version is quick and easy to make.

100 g sugar
4 cloves
½ cinnamon stick
400 ml water
1 small orange, sliced
1 small lemon, sliced
1 bottle full-bodied red wine

PUT THE SUGAR, spices and water in a saucepan and bring to the boil. Add the orange and lemon slices, stir and leave to stand for 10 minutes.

POUR IN THE WINE and heat without boiling. Ladle into glasses, leaving the solids in the pan, and serve straight away.

Egg nog

SERVES 8

Here's a rather forgotten British drink. Try it and see what you're missing.

300 ml milk
3 eggs, separated
4–5 tbsp caster sugar
1 tsp vanilla extract
250 ml brandy
150 ml single cream

HEAT THE MILK until almost boiling. Meanwhile, whisk together the egg yolks and sugar, then gradually add the vanilla and brandy. Carefully mix in the cream, then pour in the hot milk.

WHISK THE EGG WHITES until stiff, then fold into the milk mixture and serve straight away.

Buck's fizz

SERVES 1

A great celebratory drink, this gets the festivities off to a sparkling start, and goes well with Christmas muffins (page 184).

1 part orange juice
    (freshly squeezed if possible)
2 parts champagne or other
    sparkling wine

CHILL THE INGREDIENTS for at least 2 hours. Combine them in the correct proportions in a large jug, then stir well and serve in flutes.

Mango mojito

SERVES 4

Bring a taste of the Caribbean to your party! The mango adds a smooth twist to the normal mojito.

2 mangoes
1 lime
1 handful mint leaves, torn
200 ml rum (white or dark)
3–4 tbsp sugar
soda water

PEEL AND STONE the mangoes. Peel the lime, leaving on as much white pith as possible. Chop both fruits.

PUT THE FRUIT and mint leaves in a jug, then use the back of a wooden spoon to mix them roughly and release the juice and flavours. Stir in the rum and sugar, and mix well.

PUT SOME ICE in 4 tall glasses, divide the mango mixture between them and top up with soda water. Stir again and serve with a straw.

Blueberry martini

SERVES 1

Ideally, this requires a cocktail shaker, but failing that, mixing the drink in a jug with the ice and then straining it will work just as well.

JUICE the blueberries.

POUR THE JUICE and the remaining ingredients into a cocktail shaker and shake well until blended and chilled.

STRAIN INTO a martini glass and serve.

1 handful of blueberries
1 shot of vodka
1 shot of crème de cassis
ice

Darling clementine

SERVES 8—10

This refreshing, fruity drink is just as tasty without the alcohol, so ideal for all those 'nominated drivers' at your party.

CHOP THE APPLES and pears. Peel the clementines or satsumas, leaving as much white pith as possible.

JUICE THE FRUITS TOGETHER. Add a dash of Cointreau, pour over ice and serve.

2 apples
2 pears
2 clementines or satsumas
dash of Cointreau
ice

MENU IDEAS

If you've followed the Christmas countdown on page 8, you'll already have planned several meals for the holiday period. If not, here are some suggestions based on the delicious recipes in this book. First courses can be served with a green salad and/or crusty bread, while main courses can be served with any of the side dishes (pages 112–133). Don't forget that you can whip up quick and tasty meals with leftovers – check out the delicious ideas on pages 134–153.

CHRISTMAS EVE LUNCH
* Butternut squash and chorizo soup
(page 12) with crusty bread
* Walnut and fig tart (page 164)

CHRISTMAS EVE DINNER
* Chicken liver and pistachio paté
(page 17)
* Smoked pork loin with saupiquet sauce
(page 74)
* Raspberry and almond trifle
(page 178)

CHRISTMAS DAY BREAKFAST
* Christmas morning muffins
(page 184)
* Buck's fizz or Darling clementine
(pages 217, 218)

CHRISTMAS DAY LUNCH
* Roast turkey and all the trimmings
(pages 38–41)
* Christmas pudding with brandy butter
(page 156)

CHRISTMAS DAY SUPPER
(YOU WON'T WANT DINNER)

* Spicy turkey fajitas (page 144)
* Turkey sandwiches with Christmas chutney (page 132)
* Christmas ice cream (page 183)

BOXING DAY LUNCH

* Maple-and-mustard-glazed ham (page 80)
* Buttery Christmas pudding (page 151)

BOXING DAY DINNER

* Fresh salmon mousse (page 28)
* Roast lamb with garlic and mushroom stuffing (page 70)
* Lemon thyme panna cotta with raspberry granita (page 167)

NEW YEAR'S EVE LUNCH

* Aubergine parmigiana (page 100)
* Sticky date and orange pudding (page 158)

NEW YEAR'S EVE PARTY

* Mulled wine (page 216)
* Darling clementine (page 218)
* Roasted nuts in rosemary and butter (page 202)
* Assorted bruschette (page 204)
* Tiger prawn blinis (page 207)
* Asparagus, broad bean and Parmesan frittata (page 205)
* Baby peppers stuffed with goats' cheese (page 212)

NEW YEAR'S DAY LUNCH

* Cheese and ham pie (page 78)
* Zabaglione (page 173)

NEW YEAR'S DAY DINNER

* Tiger prawns and feta on toast (page 30)
* Beef fillet with a walnut crust (page 57)
* Ultimate chocolate roulade (page 193)

INDEX